One Day At A Time

One Day At A Time

140 Days of Devotional Divine Dialogue

H. DeSantis Lewis, Sr

Library of Congress Control Number:		2006909884
ISBN 10:	Hardcover	1-4257-4262-9
	Softcover	1-4257-4261-0
ISBN 13:	Hardcover	978-1-4257-4262-1
	Softcover	978-1-4257-4261-4

The Scriptures used in this devotional are from the New Living Translation Bible copyright © 1996, 2004.

This book was printed in the United States of America.

To order additional copies of this book, contact:
Xlibris Corporation
1-888-795-4274
www.Xlibris.com
Orders@Xlibris.com
36770

Acknowledgments

To the ancestral spirits of
Howard Thurman * Thomas Merton
Watchman Nee * Henri Nouwen

———————

Special thanks to my loving wife, Janet, for her undying assistance in preparing these pages; to my wonderful children for sacrificing their quality time with daddy to complete this project; to the prayer warrior ministry of Lincoln Park United Methodist Church for kindling the inspiration to create this devotional; to my neighbor and prayer partner, Pastor George Williams, for praying with me and for me as I struggled to stay focused during the many days of wanting to give up; to my mothers, Katie M. Jones and Lillian B. Harris for your distant prayers and to my spiritual father, friend and mentor in the ministry, Reverend Doctor Willie Lee Henry for believing in me down through the years. This devotional in a minute way expresses my gratitude to you for your many insights and Christian character for not only what you taught me but also what you have shown me.

Yesterday is in the tomb of time
Tomorrow is in the womb of time
Today is the only bloom of time!

The Foreword

This work "One Day At A Time" is a daily discipline for the Christian who is seeking a regular spiritual encounter with the Father, the Son and the Holy Spirit. It has been constructed contextually with a simple format: **THE READING**, which comes from the Word of God; **THE REVELATION**, which comes from the Son of God and **THE RESPONSE**, which comes from a heart to God. **THE REFLECTION**, which is a time to pause and ponder the changes or challenges prompted by the Holy Spirit after every seven [7] days of reading to better serve God.

This daily discipline encourages and engages the spiritual practitioner to develop the daily habit of . . .

> PURIFICATION—cleansing one's spirit before they begin the day;
> IMITATION—conforming to the likeness of Christ as they go about the day;
> COMMUNICATION—calling on divine wisdom to sustain them during the day;
> EDIFICATION—cultivating the soul for spiritual growth at the end of the day.

The believer must not just read these words with the head but they must be meditated upon within the heart. If this practice is submitted to daily then one will begin to notice their own transformation of faith into reality and they will find themselves becoming not just a hearer but also a doer of God's Word.

This book does not seek to serve as a substitute for your communing with God. It is simply seeking to spiritually prime and provoke you to develop a daily discipline of your own.

It is our prayer after you have devotionally and deliberately engaged the eternal through this simple guide, you would have grown closer enough to the Lord to produce your own prayers and pass them on to the next generation for meditation and edification.

Much favor,

H. De Santis Lewis, Sr.

So don't worry about tomorrow,
for tomorrow will bring its own worries.
Today's trouble is enough for today.

Matthew 6:34 NLT

ONE DAY AT A TIME, SWEET JESUS

I'm only human, I'm just a man.
Help me believe in what I could be
And all that I am.
Show me the stairway, I have to climb.
Lord for my sake, teach me to take
One day at a time.
One day at a time sweet Jesus
That's all I'm asking from you.
Just give me the strength
To do everyday what I have to do.
Yesterday's gone sweet Jesus
And tomorrow may never be mine.
Lord help me today, show me the way
One day at a time. [1]

---

[1] Lyrics taken from a favorite spiritual hymn

Day 1

The Reading:

Ecclesiastes 12:13-14, "Here is my final conclusion: Fear God and obey his commands, for this is the duty of every person. God will judge us for everything we do, including every secret thing, whether good or bad."

The Revelation:

Good morning my child. As you begin this new day, I will have you to know that the ultimate and highest goal of your life is eternal union with me in Heaven. As you go about this day in thought, words or deeds be guided in spirit by this truth. In all that you do today, strive to stay on the highway that leads to Heaven. Please do not be enticed and influenced by the passing desires and temptations of this earthly life. I have blessed you with everything that you are and with everything that you possess. Whatever else I send your way, accept it, use it and enjoy it as a gift from me. As you journey through this day, please don't let mistakes and sins rob you of your peace of mind. Keep your eyes on me. Happy only are those who desire only what I want and seek to do my will. Always examine your motives in your daily words and works. Search how you may please me more and more; avoid any and everything that cause you to drift and draw away from being in fellowship with me. Remember, nothing will happen in your life today that I can't handle.

The Response:

Most gracious Lord and my God, thank you for this gift of a brand new day. I thank you also, for reminding me that I was cosmically created for eternal happiness with you in Heaven. Therefore, everything else must take a back seat in my life because if I lose Heaven, I will be losing everything. Dear Lord, I only ask that you graciously grant me the wisdom to think and speak and act each moment of this day, as you would have me to do. May I never be such a fool to forfeit my future with you or disagree with your perfect will for my life. Help me not to sin for the sake of anything or anybody. Today, I seek to live and love only for you. Amen.

Day 2

The Reading:

Philippians 3:8-10, "Yes, everything else is worthless when compared with the priceless gain of knowing Christ Jesus my Lord. I have discarded everything else, counting it all as garbage, so that I may have Christ and become one with him. I no longer count on my own goodness or my ability to obey God's law, but I trust Christ to save me. For God's way of making us right with himself depends on faith. As a result, I can really know Christ and experience the mighty power that raised him from the dead. I can learn what it means to suffer with him, sharing in his death."

The Revelation:

Good morning my child. As you begin this beautiful day and seek to drink from the many blessings that will drip from heaven's fountain—keep in mind that the closer you draw to me during this day you will encounter many difficulties that will challenge your faith. The Devil will make use of every internal and external opposition to tempt you to resist and rebel against my way. The more you seek to live for me the more the Devil will attack and assault your faith. My child, I tell you this so that you are aware of the source behind your trials. I want you to be encouraged knowing that no amount of trials can frighten you if you learn to draw strength from my suffering and death. As you meditate on my suffering throughout this day, I will empower you with supernatural strength and faith so that you will overcome all temptations. The Devil will use everything he can to make your day stressful and miserable. Be encouraged. I will not permit you to be tempted above what you can handle. As I overcame this world so will you. I will not fail you or forsake you. Nothing will happen in your life today that I can't handle.

The Response:

Most gracious Lord and Savior, I am grateful for another day on this side of Heaven. As I seek to live this day in your honor—I will not expect an easy life. No, I want to be like you as much as I am able to. I want to work like you. I want to pray like you. I want to suffer like you as much as possible. My greatest privilege for this day is living a life like yours. You suffered for me and now in living I want to work and suffer for your Kingdom. As I live out the hours of this day, I pray that my mind will reflect upon your suffering for me often and that I may grow in my desires to suffer more for you as I seek to represent the good of the cross. Amen.

Day 3

The Reading:

Luke 9:23-24, "Then he said to the crowd, "If any of you want to be my follower, you must put aside your selfish ambition, shoulder your cross daily, and follow me. If you try to keep your life for yourself, you will lose it. But if you give up your life for me, you will find true life."

The Revelation:

Good morning my child. It is imperative that you understand those who follow me never walk in darkness. You will never have to guess or wonder with me as your guide. When you follow me in your daily life you will be walking the paths to eternal life. Do not let your emotions confuse your thinking. Do not let the blinking streetlights of materialism seduce your loyalty from me. Control your foolish pride and your lust for the things in this temporal world and follow me faithfully through my word. There are many who claim to be my followers yet they are deaf to my voice. They say that I am their Lord yet they do not submit to my word and my teachings. These people are blind and they deceive themselves. They are too proud to humble themselves and thus their religion consists only of what they understand or like or find convenient. But you are to follow me today and everyday. I am the only way, and the only truth and the only life. In following me you will find the most important knowledge of life and the only true way to eternal bliss. When you submit to my teachings and follow my example in your daily life, your reward will be greater than human words can explain. Throughout this day I want you to follow me, imitate me, and learn from me and when you do, you will gain peace and make progress toward Heaven's joy. Remember, nothing will happen in your life today that I can't handle.

The Response:

Dear God, thank you for blessing me to see another day. Thank you for being my guide of true Godliness. Thank you for allowing me to follow you and imitate you on the road to eternal life. Thank you for the institution of your church which stills stands today after years of persecution and opposition. Satan has attempted time and time again to silence her and destroy her but through it all she still serves the world as a lighthouse of truth and holiness. I pray that as I go about this day that I will faithfully follow you and the teachings of your church in all matters of faith, holiness and godliness. Amen.

Day 4

The Reading:

Psalm 37:3-4, "Trust in the Lord and do good. Then you will live safely in the land and prosper. Take delight in the Lord, and he will give you your heart's desires."

The Revelation:

Good morning my child and welcome to another blessed day. My child as you move about during this day, I want you to live each moment in my presence being constantly aware of my nearness to you. The more you discipline yourself in this virtue the more I will manifest it in you. Your degree of deeper devotion in me will help you to grow in grace, in love and in kindness toward others. With this degree of deeper devotion your faults will shrink smaller and smaller and your goodness and gentleness will shine before the world. However, to grow in this devotion requires a continual and constant effort. You must press in it like a runner running up a steep hill. If you stop trying or pressing for one moment, you will lose ground . . . Without a determined and deliberate effort there can be no progress. Throughout this day do not be afraid of being inconvenienced or suffering. The way to Heaven is the way of prayer, work and much suffering. Remember, the cross of Calvary symbolizes my love. You must use this symbol as you strive to become God-like. I know it seems impossible, but a consciousness of my presence will assist you in controlling and directing your likes and dislikes. As you move throughout this day, I want you to practice acts of faith in my presence. Too many people make only a feeble attempt to grow in me to improve themselves. And when they fail repeatedly, they give up. The reason they fail is because they neglect to stay committed and connected to my spirit through daily devotions. I not only want you to develop the duty to follow my will but to trust in me every second of the day and I will bless your efforts. Remember, nothing will happen in your life today that I can't handle.

The Response:

Most Gracious and forgiving God, I thank you over and over again for this new day. I pray that you will help me become aware of your constant presence and nearness to me all day. I don't want to fail you. You ask me to trust in you and today I will start trusting in you more and more in everything I do. Grant me the grace today to become like my Saviour and imitate Him. I want to be a true child of God. I want to find daily delight in my devotion to you and forever be found faithful in my prayer life and suffering. It is my desire to see Heaven. Amen.

Day 5

The Reading:

Matthew 5:11-12 "God blesses you when you are mocked and persecuted and lied about because you are my followers. Be happy about it! Be very glad! For a great reward awaits you in heaven. And remember, the ancient prophets were persecuted, too."

The Revelation:

Good morning my child and welcome to another day created before the foundation of the world. Today I want to encourage you not to fear the insults or contempt of anyone. For that person may seem strong today but tomorrow that same person will be laid in a coffin. I want you to fear only sin and remain close to me. Human words and injuries are not as devastating as they seem. Your persecutors hurt themselves more than they hurt you. None of them shall escape my judgment. Leave it to me to deal with them as they deal demonically with you. Do not seek revenge against any of them by words or actions. At times, criticism and fault-finding from others may disenchant and discourage you; remain patient and seek my strength. It is only through me that you will find the strength to bear your trials in peace. Through out your day meditate upon this lesson and know it is good for you to experience and endure opposition; to have people think evil of you even when you mean well. This is a valuable way of gaining and growing in humility and longer suffering. My child, never forget as long as you live among humans, you will encounter misunderstandings, criticisms and mal-treatments. Different people will treat you differently. But I want you to treat everyone with kindness, gentleness and selflessness for my sake. Yes, people will think you are a fool for not seeking an eye for an eye and a tooth for a tooth but I want you to remain steadfast in praying and forgiving those who persecute you. Remember, nothing will happen in your life today that I can't handle.

The Response:

Most gracious, kind and forgiving God; once again I am thankful to meet and greet another day. I am also grateful and thankful for you lowering yourself to make up for my sins. Even as you hung on the cross you prayed for the forgiveness of my sins. I will do no less for those who persecute me. When I am mistreated and persecuted, I will remember my own sins and offer my persecutions as reparations for the sins and selfishness I am guilty of on a daily basis. Today, I pray for the spirit of truth and the wisdom of your love to follow it. Today, I will fear no one's words or insults as much as I fear my own pride. Amen.

Day 6

The Reading:

Philippians 2:12-13 "Dearest friends, you were always so careful to follow my instructions when I was with you. And now that I am away you must be even more careful to put into action God's saving work in your lives, obeying God with deep reverence and fear. For God is working in you, giving you the desire to obey him and the power to do what pleases him."

The Revelation:

Good morning my child and welcome to another consecrated day. Today I want you to learn to leave other people alone, and when you do they will leave you alone, usually. Deal with your own business and strive to do your best to please me. I know it is human nature to be curious about what is going on with others. But how can you be one hundred percent loyal to me if you are indulging in the matters of others? Unless it is your divine duty to know, what does it mean to you to be concerned about other people's business? When the time comes you will not be responsible for the actions of others. You will only have to give an account for your own thoughts, words, deeds and missions. As you go about this day leave everyone and everything else to me and make it your undivided intention to please me and grow in your own salvation. In doing this you will not only discover your true self but you will have peace in your own heart. Again, as you journey through this day, do not make the mistake of exhausting your energy and conflicting your spirit in other people affairs. Yes, offer your prayers and be a good example with your assistance when you can and then leave the rest to me. You must live your life and let others live theirs. Remember, nothing will happen in your life today that I can't handle.

The Response:

O Lord, My God, Thank you for another day. It is a blessed bonus to enjoy another sunrise. I realize more than ever that my life is a gift from you. It is a matter that concerns only you and me. Yes Lord, I understand that I must love and assist my loved ones and friends as much as I can. But, the reality is I must live and let live. I'm thanking you for teaching me how not to worry and be over-concerned about the affairs of other people. I pray that I never fall prey again as a victim of idle curiosity. I pray that I am never guilty again of talking about my neighbor and that my daily focus is consumed with pleasing you and growing in your grace. Amen.

Day 7

The Reading:

1 John 2:15-17 "Stop loving this evil world and all that it offers you, for when you love the world, you show that you do not have the love of the Father in you. For the world offers only the lust for physical pleasure, the lust for everything we see, and pride in our possessions. These are not from the Father. They are from this evil world. And this world is fading away, along with everything it craves. But if you do the will of God, you will live forever."

The Revelation:

Good morning my child and welcome to the gift of another day. It is my desire for you today to keep your senses, especially your eyes focused on me. Too many sinful thoughts and imaginations will creep into your spirit if you don't control your curiosity to see and look upon things in this world. I warn you not to allow this fault to attract you to the temptations of the world. When you learn to keep the lust of your eyes under control, you will find it easier to stay in fellowship with me. This will also prevent sinful thoughts and evil desires from disturbing your peace of mind. Too many of my children fall prey to external temptations because of the failure to control their eyes. Today, I want you to exercise that control and resist the seduction of the media, music and movies, which serve as bait for lustful temptations. I know sometimes you grow weary of my company; only because you don't enjoy what I command of you. It is then you seek to satisfy yourself by gazing upon that which you find pleasing to your eyes. I do not begrudge a reasonable change of scenery for the refreshment of your spirit but I do warn you of the satanic objective to hypnotize you with the things of this world. Do not allow yourself to become distracted from your daily goal and that is to gain Heaven. Remember, there is nothing new under the sun and by controlling your eyes you aren't missing much. Nothing will happen in your life today that I can't handle.

The Response:

O Lord, My God, I am grateful for this gift of another day. I seek to live it pleasing you and advancing toward Heaven. I ask that as I journey to and fro that you will strengthen me to stay focused on you. I desire to behold only those things that are edifying to my spirit and worthy of my attention. I pray that throughout my day I am only attracted to those things that represent your character and have eternal value. Help me to concentrate on you dear Lord and those things, which are noble in nature. This is my prayer. Amen.

The Reflection: [What I heard the Holy Spirit speaking into my spirit during the past seven days and how it changed me or challenged me].

_____

_____

_____

_____

_____

_____

_____

_____

_____

_____

_____

_____

_____

_____

_____

_____

Day 8

The Reading:

James 1:2-4 "Dear brothers and sisters, whenever trouble comes your way, let it be an opportunity for joy. For when your faith is tested, your endurance has a chance to grow. So let it grow, for when your endurance is fully developed, you will be strong in character and ready for anything."

The Revelation:

Greetings and much grace to you this morning my child. Did you know a person's true greatness is seen in adversity? Your failures, criticisms, disappointments, oppositions, suffering and setbacks are the earthly tests to show whom you really are. Prosperity and success are not always to your advantage. The highest honor or the greatest achievement you can attain on earth is to be in a right fellowship with me in all things. The best season to achieve such an honor is in the season of adversity. When things are going well with you it could tempt you to deceive yourself. It's only during the times of adversity when you are sure to seek my face and rely on my strength for security. The strength of your faith, of your hope, or your patience and of your humility can only be measured in the times of testing. It's only during adversity can you see yourself as you really are today. I want you to become truly holy. I want you to offer and submit yourself to me without any hesitation or reservation no matter what comes your way. I want you to bury your self-interest and self-seeking in my will. As you accept adversity as a spiritual shaping and cultivating of your soul, you will then begin to grow more like me and more closer to Heaven. Always remember in your adversity, nothing will happen to you that I can't handle.

The Response:

Most loving and all wise God, I thank you for waking me up to the joy and blessing of a brand new day. Throughout this day when I'm challenged to face temptations and adversities it will be for my own good. Lord, I know you know what is best for me. I pray for the wisdom and understanding to accept and embrace my adversities knowing that my trials and tests come only to make me strong and draw me closer to you. I love you Lord and whatever it takes for me to rise to the greater heights of goodness in order to gain greater glory in eternity I am willing to submit to it daily. Thank you Lord for perfecting my faith and growing and grooming me in grace. Amen.

Day 9

The Reading:

Psalm 141:3-4 "Take control of what I say, O Lord, and keep my lips sealed. Don't let me lust for evil things; don't let me participate in acts of wickedness. Don't let me share in the delicacies of those who do evil."

The Revelation:

Good morning my child. I pray that you find this new day just as favorable as the other ones. Today's lesson focuses on talking too much and listening too little. My child, please heed this revelation and meditate on it throughout your day. The person who talks too much advances very little in knowledge. No one and I mean no one has all the answers. But the one who listens will always learn more knowledge than the one who cannot control his tongue in talking. There are times to come that you will know many answers, but it will be wiser to remain silent. As a matter of fact many discussions and dialogues are not worth indulging your opinion. When you learn how to control your tongue, you are granted the grace of divine peace. My child, hear me well today, do not love to hear your own opinion too much. Be humble and honest enough to seek the advice of others when you need it. Do not place too much confidence in your own opinion and learn to hold your tongue for the sake of peace. A person who loves to hear themselves talk and very seldom listens is full of pride. Always strive to guard what you say and be quick to listen than to speak. You will cause no harm by keeping silent. It takes much humility to act in this manner. I love you and nothing will happen in your life today that I can't handle.

The Response:

O Lord, My God, I thank you daily for leading and guiding me into all truth. I pray today for the humility and the patience to listen more and speak less. I also pray for wisdom to break my silence whenever I hear teachings that are contrary to your word or that is malicious against my neighbor. Teach me O Lord to speak only when it will advance your kingdom or edify another. Show me Lord, how to be considerate and conscious of other people's feelings and opinions as long as it doesn't compromise your commandments. Dear

Lord, please grant me the grace today to love your word more than my own opinion or the arguments of others. When I do speak today, let your words be my words; let your truths be my truths. Amen.

Day 10

The Reading:

Joshua 1:9 "I command you—be strong and courageous! Do not be afraid or discouraged. For the Lord your God is with you wherever you go."

The Revelation:

Good morning my child and may the blessings of my Father be upon you all day. Today, I want you to find much confidence in me as you encounter any trial or trouble. As you trust in me, refuse to worry or be frightened by anything. If your trials were not good for you I would cancel them immediately. Today, I want you to learn how to place yourself totally in my care and fear absolutely nothing. Remember, not one thing can confront you without my consent. The Devil will come along and provoke you to compromise your trust in me. He will then appeal to your feelings or likes and dislikes thereby seeking to corrupt your understanding of right and wrong. This tactic is simply to disturb your imagination by conflicting your idea of what's true and what's false. His objective is to produce fear. Many a persons have deferred to their feelings and imaginations thus becoming a slave to fear. My child I do not want you to make such a mistake. You are to only submit to reason and faith. Listen only to my voice and follow only my word. Walk bravely with me daily and fear nothing. I am walking with you and nothing will happen in your life today that I can't handle.

The Response:

My Lord and my God, thank you for being my very present help always. As I begin this day, I begin it with the faith and confidence that I have absolutely nothing to fear or worry about. Thank you for regulating the things I can and can't handle in this life. As I go about my duties of this day, help me not to listen to the enticing voices of the enemy, which produce fear. I pray that I won't offend your grace with a lack of confidence and trust in you. I love you, I believe in you and I trust you with all that is in me. It is my prayer today for more and more faith to counter any and all fears that may come. Amen.

Day 11

The Reading:

Matthew 26:40-41 "Then he returned to the disciples and found them asleep. He said to Peter, "Couldn't you stay awake and watch with me even one hour? Keep alert and pray. Otherwise temptation will overpower you. For though the spirit is willing enough, the body is weak!"

The Revelation:

Good morning my child and welcome to another ordained day. As you go about this day, I would have you to meditate on how you can develop a more prayerful daily life. It is important that you examine all that you do in a day's time and then begin to limit some of your projects and abandon all those that are useless. As you begin to do this you'll find that you have more time to turn your attention to me. As you audit the duties of your day—you will gradually become more conscious of my presence and you will begin to speak and act differently in your daily life. That which you fear and worry about will consume you less and less. If your desire is to be close to me then you must deliberately separate yourself from useless activities and meditate on my word and me. Much of the things that you are involved in during your daily life are like iron chains around your mind. They weigh down your attention and negate you from having fruitful fellowship with me. I do not want you to be absorbed and consumed by unnecessary distractions but to stay awake spiritually and seek the company of Heaven. When your eyes seek me throughout the day and when your ears hear my voice throughout the day, you will find yourself happier and more at peace. Nothing will happen in your life today that I can't handle.

The Response:

Most gracious Lord God, I thank you for this new and anointed day. It is my desire to stay connected to you and desire only your company during this day. I pray that you will forgive me for becoming intoxicated with the things of this world that are useless to my growth in grace. Lord, help me to fear and hate whatever may come today that may draw me away from you. Teach me how to pray and meditate on your goodness throughout my day. It is my prayer today that my eyes and ears will always be tuned in and turned on to your will so that I will remain awake and aware of your presence all day. Amen.

Day 12

The Reading:

Matthew 25:41 "Then the King will turn to those on the left and say, `Away with you, you cursed ones, into the eternal fire prepared for the Devil and his demons!'"

The Revelation:

Good morning my child and many blessings as you receive this new day. I want you to think about the realities of Hell today and understand Hell was made for the devil and his angels and Heaven was made for those who honor me. When you refuse to live for Heaven then you are choosing to live without me. Anyone who doesn't follow my law and keep my commandments becomes a candidate for Hell. And if he dies in this disobedience he joins the other fallen angels in Hell. The jury, which convicts him, is his own sinful life. I only pronounce the sentence on what he has chosen for his eternal destiny. Hear me well today my child, there is nothing on earth that can compare to Hell. Hell is beyond all description and imagination. One must see it to know it. I am not lifting up any threats to you. I simply want you to beware of the fact unless you live for Heaven when you die you will go to Hell. All the sufferings known to man can never compare to the suffering of Hell. You would rather face trials on earth than to face the fires of Hell. One day in Hell is worse more than one hundred years of suffering on earth. My child, the fires of Hell will never die out. The greatest despair and torment in Hell will be the lost of all hope to have my friendship and fellowship as Saviour. If you, my child, will follow my will in your daily life, you will never need to fear Hell. Remember, nothing will happen in your life today that I can't handle.

The Response:

Most gracious Lord God, I am thankful and grateful for this new day on earth. As I live out my life during this day, I pray that you find me pleasing and obedient to your word. I don't want to be guilty of anything that may cause me to forfeit Heaven and gain Hell. Lord, I never want to hear those words, "Depart from me!" Therefore, I pray that you will grant me the grace to do my best on earth that I may see Heaven when I die. I love you Lord and I long to spend eternity with you and not apart from you. Amen.

Day 13

The Reading:

1 Peter 4:12-13 "Dear friends, don't be surprised at the fiery trials you are going through, as if something strange were happening to you. Instead, be very glad—because these trials will make you partners with Christ in his suffering, and afterward you will have the wonderful joy of sharing his glory when it is displayed to all the world."

The Revelation:

Greetings and grace be unto you my child all throughout this day. As you journey throughout this day I want you to realize that it is a privilege to suffer for my sake. When you really meditate on how much I went through for the sins of this world, you will realize what you are called and challenged to endure is very minute. You will find it much easier to bear your burdens when you consider the agony and torture of those who have gone on before you in my name. If the thoughts of how they lived and died for me doesn't make you think less of your own trials then you are guilty of thinking more of yourself than of me. My child, I will not allow anything to happen to you that is not for your eternal good. I want you to become less anxious to enjoy this earthly life and more willing to endure your trials daily for my sake. I will grant you the grace to face your disappointments, misunderstandings and controversies with greater resignation and peace. I do not want you to expect to obtain the joy of Heaven's happiness by a life of ease and contentment in this life. As hard as this may sound, suffering is a privilege when it is encountered for my sake. My gifts of peace and patience will help you to grasp and embrace this teaching. Remember, nothing will happen in your life today that I can't handle.

The Response:

My Lord and My God, thank you for waking me to another glorious morning. As I live out this day, I pray that whatever trials or suffering come my way that I may meet them with the peace and patience of Heaven. I pray that I may be forever reminded throughout this day of your suffering and the sufferings of the saints. I pray for the opportunity to prove my unselfish love of God and that I may realize and recognize suffering for Christ is a privilege. As I am confronted by adversity today let me find joy in embracing it as a bonus for what you suffered for me. I love you Lord and I want to please you in all that I say and do. Amen

Day 14

The Reading:

Romans 7:15-18 "I don't understand myself at all, for I really want to do what is right, but I don't do it. Instead, I do the very thing I hate. I know perfectly well that what I am doing is wrong, and my bad conscience shows that I agree that the law is good. But I can't help myself, because it is sin inside me that makes me do these evil things. I know I am rotten through and through so far as my old sinful nature is concerned. No matter which way I turn, I can't make myself do right. I want to, but I can't."

The Revelation:

Greetings and grace to you this morning, my child. Today I want you to become familiar with the struggle that goes on between your flesh and your spirit. Your flesh is deeply selfish and does not seek that which is holy and healthy for you. Your flesh will try to enjoy everything on earth and still gain Heaven. Even when and where sin is involved, your flesh will make excuses and look for reasons to favor itself. Your spirit on the other hand seeks to satisfy my will. Your flesh hates to be restrained. It desires to do and follow its own will. Your spirit wrestles against your flesh to please me in everything and in every way. Be watchful for the flesh, for it loves honor and respect whereas your spirit only accepts honor in my name. Your spirit recognizes and realizes without me, you are nothing. The flesh constantly fights to avoid shame and insults. When your spirit is in control it doesn't mind shame or ridicule because it remembers what I had to submit to for your salvation. The flesh will always desire ease and comfort and not suffering. Your spirit will strive to keep laboring to build you up in my grace and to move you into spiritual maturity. My child I appeal to you not to yield to the desires of the flesh but become more and more eager daily to walk in my spirit. Nothing will happen in your life today that I can't handle.

The Response:

Most holy and gracious God, I am eternally grateful for the blessing of a brand new day. I am forever aware that without you my being could not be possible. As I strive to honor you today in thoughts, words and deeds I ask for strength not to yield to the desires of my flesh. I desire to operate obediently out of my spirit and to feed my spirit throughout the day with thoughts of you and your word. I pray that I will follow only what you desire for me. When my flesh is seduced by sin, I pray for spiritual strength to counter act it. Lord, I yield to you to lead me throughout this day in spirit and in truth. Amen

The Reflection: [What I heard the Holy Spirit speaking into my spirit during the past seven days and how it changed me or challenged me].

_____

_____

_____

_____

_____

_____

_____

_____

_____

_____

_____

_____

_____

_____

_____

Day 15

The Reading:

Romans 8:10-18 "Since Christ lives within you, even though your body will die because of sin, your spirit is alive because you have been made right with God. The Spirit of God, who raised Jesus from the dead, lives in you. And just as he raised Christ from the dead, he will give life to your mortal body by this same Spirit living within you . . . Yet what we suffer now is nothing compared to the glory he will give us later."

The Revelation:

Good morning my child; peace and blessings shall be yours all day. Too many people follow me for selfish reasons. They don't love me or serve me for me but for what they think they can gain. Many a persons desire my Kingdom but very few desire my cross! Look at how many wish to rejoice with me and then look at how many who are willing to suffer for me. As long as they don't experience any trouble; as long as I am blessing them with gifts and favor, they are willing to bless me. However when the hardships or trouble come they complain against me. I want you to love me not for my gifts but for me. Please don't follow me for what you can get but for what you can give. My child, my love for you is unconditional. There is nothing or no one greater than my love for you. You must begin to experience loving me with that kind of love. A love and suffering that places me above your own comfort and desires. If you follow me for who I am and not for what you can gain from me nothing will be withheld from you on earth or in Heaven. Remember nothing will happen in your life today that I can't handle.

The Response:

My Lord and my Saviour, I thank you for keeping me through the night and blessing me with another day. My Lord, I desire to serve you and to submit to you whole heartedly—without any self interest or motive. You deserve all I am and all I have. I pray that the words of St. Ignatius will become my words. "Lord, teach me to serve you as you deserve, teach me to give and not count the cost, teach me to fight and not heed the wounds, teach me to labor and not seek rest, teach me to give and not seek any reward except to know that I am doing your will." Lord, may my suffering and my love be payment for your unending grace all throughout this day. Amen.

Day 16

The Reading:

Psalm 8:3-4 "When I look at the night sky and see the work of your fingers, the moon and the stars you have set in place, what are mortals that you should think of us, mere humans that you should care for us?"

The Revelation:

Good morning my child; may grace and peace be yours throughout this day. There is nothing that I have created or called into being so small or unimportant that it does not in some way reflect or represent my wisdom and infinite goodness. I created the heavens and the earth to serve and provide for mankind. There are angels appointed and on duty to serve and assist my people. If you strive to live as I desire and behave in a way that is pleasing to me, you shall one day share in the perfect happiness of paradise. Throughout your day I want you to take a good look around your environment and notice the fact that my creation was established to help you live a good and godly life. Everything and everybody that exist in your immediate surroundings are gifts from me to you with a divine and definite purpose. All things, not just some of the things are in your life for my good reasons. In one way or another they were created to help you advance toward the glory of my Kingdom. As you go about this day I want you to reject and resist anything and anyone that may tempt you to question my creation or prevent anything that I have placed in your environment to aid you in living a holy and useful life. If you would employ my creation in an intelligent manner you would find it enjoyable and pleasant until I return for you. Remember, nothing will happen in your life today that I can't handle.

The Response:

O Lord, how excellent and marvelous is thy name in all the earth. I am grateful to see another day on this side of the grave. As I marvel and look upon the beauty of your creation today—I will know that it is just a tiny reflection and replica of your perfect kingdom in paradise. I pray that I will never abuse your creation or take for granted those persons you have divinely placed in my life for my own good. I pray as I live out the moments of this day that I will be only attracted to the good things that exist on earth and not the distractions that lead into sin. Lord, grant me the favor to appreciate your created examples of heaven on earth. Amen.

Day 17

The Reading:

James 4:8 "Draw close to God, and God will draw close to you. Wash your hands, you sinners; purify your hearts, you hypocrites."

The Revelation:

Good morning my child and welcome to another day made by my Father. Rejoice and be glad. I want you to learn to talk to me as a child talks with a parent. Do not allow any barriers to come between us. I know at times you will find it easier to talk to human beings than it is to talk to me. But no one else knows you better than me. No one else understands you better than me. No one else loves you better or more than me. You can never find the kind of sympathy and appreciation I have for you in any one else. I want you to know when you draw close to me you will never walk alone. I will always be with you ready to share your burdens and help solve your problems. I will walk with you every step. No one and I mean no one is capable of giving you this kind of perfect friendship except me. I even know you better than you know yourself. So do not treat me like a passing stranger. I am your eternal and ever present friend. You can have perfect confidence in my love and in my mercy. All the human affection and attention on earth cannot compare to my unconditional love for you. I am with you and will be with you every moment of this day if you would just draw near to me and trust my friendship. Do not let sin separate you from Me. Cling to me and depend on me for every living breath. Nothing will happen in your life today that I can't handle.

The Response:

My God from glory, great is your faithfulness. Thank you for watching over me as I slept and for waking me to receive the dawning of a brand new day. I thank you for being my friend and my closest companion as I move about this planet. I want to remain close to you and always in a right fellowship with you. Throughout this day I desire to prove my love and friendship with you by my actions. Grant me the grace and the strength to resist anything or anyone that may seek to come between us. I need you by my side all day. Lord, I don't ever want to lose the perfect friend I have in you. Walk with me and talk with me throughout this day's journey. Amen.

Day 18

The Reading:

Acts 14:22 "Where they strengthened the believers. They encouraged them to continue in the faith, reminding them that they must enter into the Kingdom of God through many tribulations."

The Revelation:

Good morning my child and blessings be unto you all during the day. My child, you will have to face many trials and tribulations while in this life. During these times, I will send angels to console and comfort you. Please do not look for or expect lasting contentment in this life. There are going to be many days when you are going to have to do some things you don't want to do and give up a lot of things you will desire. I am forewarning you so that you are prepared to fight the daily struggles of trouble. This you must do and go through to gain Heaven. Without a fight; without a battle; without trials and tribulations there can be no triumph. If you refuse to fight you only deprive yourself of the final glory, which is to come. If you fight on; if you suffer successfully; if you meet your trials with faith, there is a glorious crown awaiting you in Heaven. It can only be attained and appreciated by enduring the daily battles of life. Please be assured that I, your Lord and friend, will march before you, will fight with you and at times, fight for you. As you go about this day be ready and on guard to follow me fearlessly and faithfully. If you abandon my way, and me you will become your own worst enemy. Your spiritual greatness or littleness will depend upon how you confront your battles. Nothing will happen in your life today that I can't handle.

The Response:

My God and my Lord, thank you for your grace and your mercy. Thank you for your sustaining power in times of trouble and trials. Thank you for your example of suffering as you endured the cross for my sake. You showed the kind of faith, hope and love that you desire of me in this life. I pray that I will no longer seek to just avoid sin and temptation but I will confront them with an eagerness to grow in your grace. Help me to understand that my battles are times of spiritual growth and advancement toward Heaven. I love you Lord and I want to please you and find favor with you. Amen.

Day 19

The Reading:

2 Timothy 3:16-17 "All Scripture is inspired by God and is useful to teach us what is true and to make us realize what is wrong in our lives. It straightens us out and teaches us to do what is right. It is God's way of preparing us in every way, fully equipped for every good thing God wants us to do."

The Revelation:

Good morning my child and may my spirit be with you all throughout the day. Spiritual reading and reflecting upon that which you have read is profitable for your growth and development. My word has been inspired and written to help you gain a greater understanding and appreciation of my will. When you read my word do not do so to impress others but to empower and impress yourself. Read my word daily so that you may learn my way of thinking and that you may be able to rightly divide my truths when necessary. Yes, I inspired the authors of my word but I did not inspire many of the translators who now speak in my name. I want you to consult me for discernment to detect any errors or inaccuracies when it comes to studying my word. Also be advised that the scriptures alone will not guide you into eternal life. Some of them are written simply and some profoundly and not always easy to comprehend. This is why there are many opinions and beliefs about my word. Because of these differences of opinions many of my followers are separated from each other. I do not want you to submit to any doctrine or belief except that which is predicated upon my unadulterated word. Follow the true light, which shines through my church. The church has been given the authority under the guidance of my Holy Spirit to teach and preach my word. When you hear the word, you hear me. Whenever you are in doubt, don't worry; call on me and I will grant you wisdom to understand. Remember, nothing will happen in your life today that I can't handle.

The Response:

Dear God, my Father, thank you for blessing me to see another day and for the opportunity to grow closer to you. I ask that you grant me wisdom to read and reflect upon your word. I ask that you would anoint my hearing and understanding that I may discern the difference between your word and someone's human opinion. I desire only to share and apply your precepts and truths in my daily life. I pray that as I study your word and yield to the teachings of your Holy Spirit that I will be divinely directed in all matters of faith and morality. I pray for a daily dose of wisdom, knowledge and understanding as I feast and fellowship with your word. Amen.

Day 20

The Reading:

Micah 7:5-6 "Don't trust anyone—not your best friend or even your wife! For the son despises his father. The daughter defies her mother. The daughter-in-law defies her mother-in-law. Your enemies will be right in your own household."

The Revelation:

Good morning my child and welcome to another wonderful day to grow in grace. The more you study and grow in my word the more you will learn what I teach is only the wise thing to do. I am simply suggesting that you trust people and things according to their true merit. When you place the wrong trust in people and things you encounter in your daily life you offend me and limit me to second place. How would you like to have counterfeit money for real money? Neither should you be satisfied with the false value or worth of any person or thing. Learn this lesson and you will never again prefer anything or anyone to me. When you place more trust in people and things you are sinning for the sake of that thing and putting more into it than it deserves. When you do that you are choosing a passing satisfaction over the lasting joy and peace that I prefer you to have. Don't continue to deceive yourself, let your first interest be my will and merely trust things and people as much as they deserve. Not only will you avoid any mistakes with your love and loyalty but your affection will be broadened and purified; your selfish motives will become weaker and rarer and you will develop into the person I destined you to become. Nothing will happen in your life today that I can't handle.

The Response:

My God, praise and blessings to you for granting me the bonus of another beautiful day. Thank you for watching over me last night and for waking me up this morning. I pray today for wisdom and insight on keeping people and things in proper perspective. I want to value the people and things in my life for what they are worth. No more and no less. I desire to give you first place in my life in all that I do. You are the best and greatest friend I can have. I place all my trust and loyalty in you and your word. Do not let my heart control my head but let your Holy Spirit govern my unreasoning desires for people and things. Thus, I will have peace and joy. Amen.

Day 21

The Reading:

Matthew 15:7-9 "You hypocrites! Isaiah was prophesying about you when he said, these people honor me with their lips, but their hearts are far away. Their worship is a farce, for they replace God's commands with their own man-made teachings."

The Revelation:

Good morning my child and blessings and peace are yours today. It is a sad sight for me to witness how my children confess one thing with their lips but their lives portray something totally different. It is spiritually dangerous to pledge your allegiance to me and then live contradictory to your pledge. Please pay close attention how you represent your relationship with me. Each day your life and loyalty in serving me should improve. You are not just called to avoid evil but you are to do good. The one thing that grieves my spirit is to see how half-hearted and negligent my people are. Many of them quickly lose their devotion to me and grow tired of pursuing the higher holiness. They thus become spiritual lazy and fall into spiritual tepidity. My child, I want your desire to grow closer to me and in the ways of my word to increase every day. Occasional thinking about me and keeping my commandments is not healthy for our relationship. Your head, your heart and hands must all be on one accord if you are to truly be a follower of me. There are many who love associating with my name but they refuse to submit to the labors, the sorrows and the hardships that come along with it. Please do not live as a hypocrite but be willing to serve and to suffer as an ambassador of Heaven. Let your lips and your life honor me. Nothing will happen in your life today that I can't handle!

The Response:

Most gracious Lord and Saviour, thank you for the blessing of another day and for the opportunity to represent you in spirit and in truth. It is my desire to live each hour of this day honoring you with my lips and my life. I pray that I am not guilty of living half-hearted or spiritually lazy. Every opportunity that I have today I will exercise my spiritual discipline through prayer, studying the word and serving others in your honor. I ask that you would grant me the grace to model a holy life for you. I want to do whatever I need to do to avoid living a hypocritical lifestyle. Amen.

The Reflection: [What I heard the Holy Spirit speaking into my spirit during the past seven days and how it changed me or challenged me].

Day 22

The Reading:

1 Peter 5:8-9 "Be careful! Watch out for attacks from the Devil, your great enemy. He prowls around like a roaring lion, looking for some victim to devour. Take a firm stand against him, and be strong in your faith. Remember that your Christian brothers and sisters all over the world are going through the same kind of suffering you are."

The Revelation:

Good morning my child, welcome to another day to represent my holiness. My child, my child please be aware that the Devil never sleeps and that the desires of your flesh is yet alive. This means that you must always be on guard against a battle with the enemies within you that never rest. Your old self (enemy) is opposed to everything that is good and godly. Your old enemy never gets tired of tempting you to sin. All day and all night, he sets snares and traps for you hoping that you will be seduced and seized by his bait. Be forever watchful for these traps and temptations. This is why you must pray continually for my grace and guidance to overcome the enemy's tricks and tactics. No one on the planet is completely safe from these temptations. Why? Because the source of your temptation is within you. The blind tendency of your faith will always be on the search to satisfy its animalistic appetite. Not even your intellect or reason can negate this sinful drive and self-favoring urge without considering what is true or what is right. Thus, when one temptation subsides another one immediately follows. As long as you are on the earth you will suffer these struggles of the flesh. The Devil's greatest ally against your spiritual welfare is the sinful self within you. If you stay close to me I will alert you to his temptations. Nothing will happen in you life today that I can't handle.

The Response:

All loving and all wise God I'm grateful to be alive to experience and enjoy another day with you. I thank you for keeping me throughout the night. My Lord and My God, I long and very deeply desire to represent and reflect your holiness in my life. Grant me the spiritual insight to recognize myself for what I really am. Let me not be blinded by my weaknesses and faults and thus fall prey to the temptations of the Devil. I pray for your guidance against any sin that may seduce me to sabotage my salvation. I pray for guidance against any trap that may endanger my journey towards eternity with you. Lord, help me to be watchful daily for the devil's tricks and on guard against my own sinful passions. I love you Lord. Amen.

Day 23

The Reading:

Psalms 34:1-3 "I will praise the Lord at all times. I will constantly speak his praises. I will boast only in the Lord; let all who are discouraged take heart. Come, let us tell of the Lord's greatness; let us exalt his name together."

The Revelation:

Good morning my child; I hope you appreciated the peaceful rest and sleep you were blessed with. All things were created and divinely designed by me. Nothing can exist in this world or the next without my power. I am the centerpiece and the source of all wisdom and truth. In your daily life I desire you to love only truth. It is the honest person; It is the person who walks daily after my word that pleases me. My child you are the work of my hands and every moment of your being depends on me for existence. I only ask that you recognize that daily and be grateful for my grace. You should never act as though you deserve the daily opportunities or the good things that come your way, that kind of attitude is prideful and a lie. My Father and I owe you absolutely nothing but you owe us everything. For every heartbeat, for every breath, for every word and for every thought you receive is a result of our blessing to you. Our generosity never ceases to come your way even when you are unworthy. Our love for you cares for your daily needs every second, every minute and every hour of every day and night. Continue to be thankful for what we send your way; not just in words alone but by your actions as well. Always seek to be humble, to be patient, to be kind and to be generous and this will be daily proof of your sincere gratitude to me. Remember nothing will happen in your life today that I can't handle.

The Response:

My Lord and my all; I am deeply thankful for another day's journey. I pray that in all that I say and do today will reflect my gratitude for all that you do for me and all that you mean to me. Lord, your grace and mercy are obvious everyday I am alive on this planet. For your gracious generosity and unconditional love I will bless and praise your name continuously throughout this day. I desire to prove my eternal gratitude not just in words but in the way I live and treat others. I will be mindful for the gift of this day and use the time afforded during the day to praise you and to please you. In all my thoughts, words, and actions I will shout "Thank you Lord." Amen.

Day 24

The Reading:

Mark 8:34 "Then he called his disciples and the crowds to come over and listen."If any of you wants to be my follower," he told them, "you must put aside your selfish ambition, shoulder your cross, and follow me."

The Revelation:

Good morning my child, may my blessings be upon you throughout this day. It is not natural or normal to desire your cross, to desire insults, to desire punishing your body because of the cross or to actually love bearing or suffering for the cross. Any one who desires and follows these practices is more than likely putting on a show to attract admiration. Without my grace and strength it is impossible to gain the victory over your weaknesses. Only through me can you gain control over your pride and temptations. Never desire the cross of suffering for show or self-exaltation. Be a good soldier and embrace your cross for no other reason than for the love of me. Your daily crosses of suffering; persecution, disappointments, opposition and setbacks can only be managed in partnership with me. Apart from me your cross will crush you and conquer you. When I feel that you can be trusted and can handle a heavier cross, I will send one your way. However, I will never burden you or ask you to bear a cross beyond your abilities and strength. The heavier the cross, though, the greater the glory and ecstasy you will have in Heaven. As you bear your daily crosses, you need only to prepare your soul daily in prayer and self-training. As you practice little acts of self-denial, I will show you how to draw closer to me in patience and self-forgetfulness. Your self-sacrifices not your false pretenses will gain you firmer love for me and thus you will find it easier to suffer your daily trials of the cross. Nothing will happen in your life today that I can't handle.

The Response:

Most Gracious Lord Jesus and King, I am grateful for the blessing of this new day. Thank you for allowing me to witness its beauty. As I rise to take up my cross and meet any other crosses that I may be called to bear today, I pray that I will genuinely accept them for your sake only. Only by your grace and help am I aware that I can endure my daily trials. Yes, I shudder at knowing that I may have to suffer criticism, failures and pain today as my crosses but enable me to bear them under your strength as you prepare me for greater ones for the love of you. Amen.

Day 25

The Reading:

1 Corinthians 10:13 "But remember that the temptations that come into your life are no different from what others experience. And God is faithful. He will keep the temptation from becoming so strong that you can't stand up against it. When you are tempted, he will show you a way out so that you will not give in to it."

The Revelation:

Good morning my child and welcome to another ordained day. When temptations confront you and keep returning to you day after day do not become discouraged. I am always near you ready to assist you and grant you my grace to keep you from sinning. Never fear or worry but keep your courage and be prepared to keep fighting and resisting your temptations. No one is lost because they are tempted. Your first step towards safety is recognizing your weakness and need to depend on me. Next, do not grow despondent by temptation keep your mind on pleasing me and honoring me. No temptation can make you sin. Many persons while making their greatest progress find themselves slipping. Do not fret because of this; I look at your intentions and efforts and by them I judge your loyalty to me. My child, I want you to keep on trying for my sake. Do not consider yourself a failure because you feel like one. Be brave and follow me daily in your efforts. Yes, temptations are going to come and go. Some may even linger around for hours or days but, I want you to place your hope and trust in my mercy and I will grant you the victory. I have over come this world and with me you shall win the daily battles of temptations for Heaven. Nothing will happen in your life today that I can't handle.

The Response:

My Lord and my Saviour, I greet you with thanksgiving and praise this morning. Another day is a testament of your grace and mercy for me. Lord, I pray today when I'm confronted with temptations that I will seek your strength and resolve as to what to do. I never want to displease you or dishonor you with my behavior. If I shall fail in a moment of weakness help me to realize

I am not a failure. Help me never to despair. I know my sins are not greater than your mercy. Grant me the wisdom and power to resist all sins in the future. Help me to fight and flee all temptations today and not yield to sin. Lord, I shall trust unconditionally in your love and goodness for all things. Amen.

Day 26

The Reading:

Psalms 51:1-3 "Have mercy on me, O God, because of your unfailing love. Because of your great compassion, blot out the stain of my sins. Wash me clean from my guilt. Purify me from my sin. For I recognize my shameful deeds they haunt me day and night."

The Revelation:

Good morning my child, and welcome to another blessed day. I hope that you will yield to my teaching regarding what is best for you in your daily living. I want you to think of your sins with great displeasure and sorrow. Please don't ever think of yourself as somebody because of your deeds. To put it simply, you are a sinner. Whenever you fail to stay close to me you tend to do what is wrong and fall into sin. You are much weaker than you think. Never take pride in yourself but humble yourself before me. I don't want you to fear anything but your sins. Always run from them as much as you run from anything else. Your sins should be the one thing that displease and disturb you more than anything else. Always consider the sins you have committed and fear my judgment to come. Be honest with yourself; face the truth about yourself and know that only my love can spare you from the flames of Hell. My father loves an honest person. If you hide the truth about your sinful ways, neither my Father nor I will be pleased. All I ask of you today is to begin to fight vigorously against your sins. My child, being a sinner is not the worst condition. The worst condition is remaining a sinner. My Father loves a repentant sinner and one who honestly makes a daily effort to resist and rid himself of any faults. Be strong in your endeavor to live holy and know that nothing will happen in your life today that I can't handle.

The Response:

Greetings Lord God, and to you be the glory for all that you have done. I am grateful for this new day and the opportunity to live holy for you. I want to thank you for making me aware of my faults and not dealing with me according to my sins. Lord, I want to prove my discontent and sorrow for any sins that displeases you. Show me what saddens you and I will begin to campaign against it. I may never get rid of it but I will keep trying and trying everyday to subdue it. Lord, I don't have much to offer you but my honest daily effort to prove to you how much I love you and my sorrow for hurting your heart when I sin. Have mercy on me. Amen.

Day 27

The Reading:

Matthew 6:33 "And he will give you all you need from day to day if you live for him and make the Kingdom of God your primary concern."

The Revelation:

Good morning my child; grace, peace and favor be with you today. Many a persons are faced with choices in their lives. Every day people are making big and small; important and not so important choices. When they choose one thing they usually give up another. No one can have everything they desire. There will be times you will have to make a choice over one thing or another. In this life, you will have to make many choices. There will be something that will draw you away from me. If you desire eternal salvation you must turn away from those seductions and distractions. I desire you to make me your highest goal every minute of the day. Strive to make me your choice without even thinking about your own convenience or inconvenience. When you seek me first as your daily priority you will find perfect peace and lasting joy of the spirit. When you seek me first, you will find that I am more than any accomplishment; I am more than any human accolade; I am more than any earthly satisfaction. Only your own misguided self-interest can cause you to forfeit this holy satisfaction. As you limit your love and daily desire for me, you will increase your spiritual poverty and discontent. The less you seek my perfect will and fellowship the more you harm yourself. My companionship is priceless and my friendship will endure forever. Not even death can dissolve it. The choice is yours. Nothing will happen in your life today that I can't handle.

The Response:

Most gracious and merciful God, thank you for the blessing of a brand new day. Thank you for keeping me throughout the night. As I began this new day, my first priority is to seek to make you my highest choice. Lord, I am willing to abandon and avoid all things and foolish ideas to be in fellowship with you. This is the greatest choice and privilege I can ever make. I want to be in a close companionship with you. Make me humble enough to follow your directions, unselfish enough to forsake my own satisfaction and wise enough to choose your friendship. Today, I prefer your companionship over and above everything else. Amen.

Day 28

The Reading:

1 Samuel 16:7-8 "But the Lord said to Samuel, "Don't judge by his appearance or height, for I have rejected him. The Lord doesn't make decisions the way you do! People judge by outward appearance, but the Lord looks at a person's thoughts and intentions. Then Jesse told his son Abinadab to step forward and walk in front of Samuel. But Samuel said, "This is not the one the Lord has chosen.""

The Revelation:

Good morning my child; may my peace and presence comfort you throughout the day. Respect by others is simply the fear of being criticized or corrected. I want you to live your life in my company and do not give too much thought about what other people may think or say about you. As long as you have a clear and clean conscience, the thoughts and words of others can neither hinder or help; add to or subtract from your true value. You are not a better person because people praise you; you are not a bad person because people find fault with you. You are who you are because I created you. Your value to me does not depend on the feeble judgment of people. I look upon your heart. I look upon your sincere intentions and efforts. Other people judge you based upon their likes and dislikes or by their own vanity and pride. I want you to imitate my servant Paul. Remember, he tried to please everyone, yet he made no account of what people thought about him. He knew it was impossible to satisfy everyone. Be like Paul and put your life in my hands and leave your judgment to me. Never neglect to do good nor perpetrate any wrong because you fear the criticism and ridicule of others. Always do what is right and the truth will defend you. I see it all. Nothing will happen in your life today that I can't handle.

The Response:

Dearest God, my father and true judge. I am very grateful for another day of life. Thank you for watching over me as I go about this day I only desire to please you and not give way to the criticisms of others. I pray that I will never neglect to do good or commit a wrong because I fear being mocked or hurt by others. Only you are holy. Only you are worthy to pass judgment. I will no longer concern myself with what others think of me. Only you, my Lord and my God, really knows me and my heart. Never again, will I allow the opinions of others define me or turn me away from your holy will. Search me O God and know me! Amen.

The Reflection: [What I heard the Holy Spirit speaking into my spirit during the past seven days and how it changed me or challenged me].

_____

_____

_____

_____

_____

_____

_____

_____

_____

_____

_____

_____

_____

_____

_____

_____

Day 29

The Reading:

Revelation 21:1-2, "Then I saw a new heaven and a new earth, for the old heaven and the old earth had disappeared. And the sea was also gone. And I saw the holy city, the new Jerusalem, coming down from God out of heaven like a beautiful bride prepared for her husband."

The Revelation:

Good morning my child and receive this new day as a gift from my Father. Today as you go about your daily duties, I want you to think often about Heaven. As much as possible do not let anything dim your vision of your last and highest goal. Your thoughts and visions of Heaven will bring you peace in adversity and joy in times of trouble. In Heaven, you are going to have more than you have ever desired to have and much more than you could ever imagine. In Heaven, you will never know the end of joy. In Heaven, you will never be tormented by the fear of losing what you love. In Heaven, you will always have what you want and always enjoy the best. In Heaven, no one will complain about you. There will be no one to resist you or spoil your happiness. You will experience and enjoy the company and fellowship of my Father and me forever and ever. You will be blessed with a glory undreamed of by mortals and a reward unheard of for your victories over temptations and trials on earth. Heaven will be your eternal abode where the angels will praise you for your allegiance and loyalty to me. No human language can ever describe heaven. Every moment you live holy and righteous for me will bring you closer and closer to inheriting your home in Heaven. Nothing will happen in your life today that I can't handle.

The Response:

O Lord my God and Keeper. Thank you for this gift of another day. I desire to live it to the fullest for you and in your presence. As I think about Heaven, it arouses my desire even more to live a life pleasing to you and worthy to be rewarded eternity in Heaven with you. I realize now more than ever that I was created for eternal glory. I pray for the grace and strength to resist any evil that will come between me and my holy desire for Heaven. When my earthly life is over, I look forward to being welcomed into your presence. Everyday, I'm striving to make Heaven my home. Amen.

Day 30

The Reading;

2 Corinthians 10:3-5, "We are human, but we don't wage war with human plans and methods. We use God's mighty weapons, not mere worldly weapons, to knock down the Devil's strongholds. With these weapons we break down every proud argument that keeps people from knowing God. With these weapons we conquer their rebellious ideas, and we teach them to obey Christ."

The Revelation:

Good morning my child and welcome to another ordained day. I do not want you to be troubled when you are visited by strange thoughts. There is nothing wrong with you when your mind tends to shift from holy desires and then back to foolish thoughts. As long as you don't act and are truly displeased with them, I will not hold them against you. Thus, you will earn great merits with me for refusing to consent to them. The Devil is permitted to roam over the earth. His ambition is to perpetually try to kill any desire you have for me. Yes, he will attempt in a variety of ways to distract and draw your holy discipline away from me. He can only have power over you and hurt you only if you submit to his suggestions. The Devil studies you daily to learn where you are the weakest. The Devil takes advantage of that knowledge and suggests thoughts to cause weariness and despair in you. His motive is to pull you away prayer, reading my Word and doing any good work for the kingdom. If you decide to stand by me and yield to my spirit, the Devil will be helpless against you. Despise the Devil and fear him not. Meditate on my Word day and night and your thoughts will be pure and holy. The Devil can't make you do anything. He can only suggest it. Nothing will happen in your life today that I can't handle.

The Response:

Dearest God of mercy and love; I am grateful for another day to be alive and with another opportunity to serve you. I ask that you will anoint my mind and thoughts that they may represent your thoughts and your ways. When my mind become cloudy and confuse with anxieties and evil tendencies, I pray that you will grant me the wisdom of your grace to fix my eyes on you. It is my desire to meditate on your Word day and night and to think only on those things, which are noble, pure and holy. Help me to drink only from your well of wisdom and expose my mind only on those things, which please you. Teach me how to guard my thoughts. Teach me how to seek only your truth and to keep the Devil at bay. Amen.

Day 31

The Reading:

2 Corinthians 13:5 "Examine yourselves to see if your faith is really genuine. Test yourselves. If you cannot tell that Jesus Christ is among you, it means you have failed the test."

The Revelation:

Good morning my child and welcome to another blessed day. As you live in daily preparation to gain Heaven, I do not want you to live like a robot nor do I want you to just follow some religious routine in fear of Me finding fault with you. Yes, I am coming but my coming is because I love you; because you need me and because I want to come. As you prepare for my coming and for eternal life, constantly examine how you are living and in what ways are you unworthy of my love and my grace. Examine your faults and resolve immediately to do something about them. For me, love means action; a determine and definite action where it is needed. Again, avoid being routine and just religious. Try to make your daily communion with me a grand occasion. Put some variety in the time we spend together. Don't always say the same prayers. Experience me in different ways daily. One day meditate on my Word. On another day say your prayers aloud. On another day read books that esteem me. On another day, sing songs that motivate your spirit. Always examine yourself and your sins. Confess and repent of any behavior that does not please me. I love you and long to receive you into my kingdom for all of eternity. Nothing will happen in your life today that I can't handle.

The Response:

O Lord, My God, I am truly grateful for the blessing of another day. As I begin to engage this day, I want to express my thanksgiving and appreciation to you for your grace and mercy. I ask during this day that you help me to examine my life and my love for you. You deserve more than some routine prayers or religious jargon. I want to experience and express my love for you in different ways. I want to approach you daily with a living and exciting spirit. Teach me, Lord, to scrutinize my sins and evaluate my love for you daily. You deserve the best I have to offer in spirit, in behavior and in love. I don't ever want to receive you with a dull and thoughtless spirit. Let my daily prayers and habit of thanksgiving be full of fervor, flavor, and variety. Amen.

Day 32

The Reading:

Romans 12:1-2 "And so, dear brothers and sisters, I plead with you to give your bodies to God. Let them be a living and holy sacrifice—the kind he will accept. When you think of what he has done for you, is this too much to ask? Don't copy the behavior and customs of this world, but let God transform you into a new person by changing the way you think. Then you will know what God wants you to do, and you will know how good and pleasing and perfect his will really is."

The Revelation:

Good morning my child and may the favor of my Father follow you throughout the day. Your growth in holiness depends much on my grace and your determination as a disciple. You will always have my grace at your disposal but its your will that shifts and changes. If you would discipline yourself to pray and study my Word daily, even sacrificially you would find your strength growing stronger and stronger to do my will. My child, it is not enough to resolve to do good in the morning. You must constantly and deliberately recall and renew your resolutions throughout the day. Continuously, examine and evaluate your resolve and when you have fallen short, start over. Anyone can make resolutions to live holy but keeping them and renewing them is the discipline of a real Christian. If you become discouraged and fear starting over when you fail, it is only because you don't understand the daily spiritual struggles going on in your life. It is not a sin to fail and begin again. I do not judge you by your failures but by your efforts. Be honest with yourself and you will be humble. Seek my grace and keep on trying. As you continue to renew your mind, you will discover your faults slowly disappearing. My grace will never fail you and I will never abandon you. Nothing will happen in your life today that I can't handle.

The Response:

Most gracious Lord God, I am indeed grateful for the blessing of this new day. Beholding the rising sun is a testament of your favor in my life. I pray throughout this day that I will not only renew my resolution to live holy but I will also fight and resist any personal faults that seek to cause me to compromise my covenant with you. If I should fail or falter in any way today, it is my desire to constantly renew my efforts to please you. I love you Lord and I want to be found holy and acceptable by you. Amen.

Day 33

The Reading:

John 14:27 "I am leaving you with a gift—peace of mind and heart. And the peace I give isn't like the peace the world gives. So don't be troubled or afraid."

The Revelation:

Good morning my child and may the peace of Heaven inhabit your spirit today. My child today I desire you to experience my perfect peace. There are many who yearn this peace but very few are willing to do what it takes to obtain it. My will and My Word are the only doors to peace. I only bless those who are humble and generous with their neighbor with my peace. To acquire my peace and be assured of it daily, seek to bless others above yourself; always seek the lowest place and let others be esteem before you. When you give your all for all and do not discriminate with your offering then my peace will flow in abundance within you. Perfect peace is the tranquility that comes from order. Let me govern your life and learn to do things my way and you shall have this peace. Who knows better than me how you should live? Therefore, if you want this daily peace then you must follow my commands. If you are not faithful in keeping my commands then you will forfeit this peace. You already know that I will never burden you beyond what you can bear. You already know that I love you with an agape' love and will never impose harm onto you willingly. Now you must be convinced that I will take care of you and protect you with my grace. Now submit to my will and you will possess the priceless treasure of my eternal peace. Nothing will happen in your life today that I can't handle.

The Response:

God of mercy, God of peace, I give holy thanks for this gift of another day. Your grace has kept me. As I begin this day and go about my duties, I pray that your perfect peace will be my constant companion. Teach me today, dear Lord, how to free my mind of frustrations and meditate upon those things that stand in agreement with your peace. Teach me and impress on me that when my life contradicts your will for me I am my own worst enemy. Convince me throughout this day beyond all doubt that my greatest advantage comes from ordering my life with your Word. And only then will I know that peace I yearn for daily. That peace everyone seeks but few possess. Lord, I know you only desire the best for me and no longer will I resist it. Bless me with you peace. Amen.

Day 34

The Reading:

1 John 4:19-21, "We love each other as a result of his loving us first. If someone says, "I love God," but hates a Christian brother or sister, that person is a liar; for if we don't love people we can see, how can we love God, whom we have not seen? And God himself has commanded that we must love not only him but our Christian brothers and sisters, too."

The Revelation:

Good morning my child and may you receive this new day with the spirit of joy and peace. Let's talk about love. I mean true divine love and godly love. Many affections or feelings are mistaken for true love until it is put to the test or trial. Only time and tests will prove how genuine your love is for me. Both of these proctors of love, time and tests are sent to watch you daily and to evaluate your sincerity about your love. I pray that you do not fail me in your daily activities. Do not allow your vows to me grow cold but keep them renewed throughout the day. If not, when you are faced with adversities throughout the day you will seek a quick relief instead of seeking me for comfort and strength. Throughout this day you will experience a number of situations to prove your love for me. When the test and trials of difficulties, disappointments, and discomforts come your way, do not fret or fear or become discouraged. Do what you can to resolve them and if they are beyond your strength and control accept them as my will to cultivate you. Just like you are pleased when pleasant things come be also willing to accept the challenges I permit to come your way. Keep your eyes on my love and my purpose for you. Do not be ashamed to serve others and never let them cause you to forsake your love for me. I want you to bless me with your love. I want you to never stop loving me or your neighbor for my sake. Nothing will happen in your life today that I can't handle.

The Response:

Oh Lord, My Lord; the Lord of life, love, and mercy. I am abundantly grateful for this new day; a day to live and love for you in all that I do. Lord, as I live out this day let my attitude, my desires and my actions be a testament how much I love you. As I live out this day, let my love for my brothers and sisters be a testament how much I love them through you. May I do nothing to contradict my love for you or my neighbor. May my daily life prove beyond all doubt my unselfish and uncompromising love for you. I love you and I am eternally grateful for your love. Amen.

Day 35

The Reading:

Romans 3:23-25, "For all have sinned; all fall short of God's glorious standard. Yet now God in his gracious kindness declares us not guilty. He has done this through Christ Jesus, who has freed us by taking away our sins. For God sent Jesus to take the punishment for our sins and to satisfy God's anger against us. We are made right with God when we believe that Jesus shed his blood, sacrificing his life for us. God was being entirely fair and just when he did not punish those who sinned in former times."

The Revelation:

Good morning my child and welcome to another anointed and spirit filled day. When it comes to the grace of God, there is nothing next to God most precious to possess. When you receive God's grace, your mind receives holy thoughts, your will receive holy desires and you are constantly drawn toward those things that are holy. This is a special gift. Never oppose this grace. Never take this grace for granted. Cherish it; follow it and abide in it faithfully. By doing this you will prove your love and loyalty to me. With this grace, your prayer life, your self-denial, and your spiritual life will grow more and more. Little by little a change will begin to take place over your thinking, your desires and over your daily action. This means not only are you justified by my grace but you are also sanctified by my grace. This means you have been set apart and are being prepared and made worthy of Heaven. No matter what you do on earth without my grace all of your deeds will not make you worthy of Heaven. Nothing you can think of is so great a gift—not miracles, not prophecy, not any other gifts. It is grace that changes a person and makes them more like me. Without grace you will remain bound to earth and ruled by your human nature. It is grace that draws you closer to God, makes you stronger against temptation and deserving of the Kingdom of Heaven. Nothing will happen in your life today that I can't handle.

The Response:

Most gracious Lord and God of all; thank you for waking me up this morning. Thank you for your grace and mercy. I know as I live out this day I will be able to do nothing unless your grace enables me, enlightens me and strengthens me to do so. Without your grace I am weak and helpless against all temptations. As I go through this day I pray that I will not neglect your grace or take it for granted. I desire to walk in your grace every hour of this day and prove myself worthy of Heaven. I am thankful for your grace and vow to turn my back on whatever seeks to deprive me of your grace. Amen.

The Reflection: [What I heard the Holy Spirit speaking into my spirit during the past seven days and how it changed me or challenged me].

_____

_____

_____

_____

_____

_____

_____

_____

_____

_____

_____

_____

_____

_____

_____

_____

_____

Day 36

The Reading:

Revelation 3:15-16, "I know all the things you do, that you are neither hot nor cold. I wish you were one or the other! But since you are like lukewarm water, I will spit you out of my mouth!"

The Revelation:

Good morning my child, I pray that you receive the sweet sleep that came to you during the evening. I would have you to know today that spiritual tepidity (that is lukewarmness) is another name for being half-hearted in your service to my Father. When you are lukewarm it doesn't mean that you avoid your kingdom duties but it means you are not excited or enthusiastic about it. A spiritual tepid person does little as possible and usually does it out of habit. In other words, that person has lost the joy of serving me. My child, when you start to grow lukewarm in your divine service, you are slipping into a dangerous condition. Your zeal and zest will dissipate and dissolve. Your soul will begin to look for comfort and consolation from the world. You will gradually contract the diseases of laziness and worldliness. These two germs will cause your spiritual death and demise. You must constantly arouse yourself through prayer, praising and meditating on my Word day and night. Keep your service for me alive and active by reaching out to others with love and hope. The mood of tepidity comes to every one from time to time but you are never to let it become a habit with you. Resist this spirit by staying in a right relationship and fellowship with me. I will keep your soul on fire. Nothing will happen in your life today that I can't handle.

The Response:

O Lord, My God I will praise your name at all times. Songs of thanksgiving will forever be upon my lips and in my heart. I want to thank you for the blessing of another day. My sleep was divine. Dear Lord, as I strive to serve you in ministry, I pray that I never lose my zeal and zest in my service for you. It is a privilege to be one of your servants and I don't want to take that privilege for granted by becoming spiritually lazy or lukewarm. Remind me daily of my inheritance if I don't give up and quit and of my damnation if I do. Lord, I don't want to ever let you down or do anything to cause you to spit me out of your mouth. I love you and desire to serve you with joy and enthusiasm until I die. Amen.

Day 37

The Reading:

Matthew 11:28-30, "Then Jesus said, "Come to me, all of you who are weary and carry heavy burdens, and I will give you rest. Take my yoke upon you. Let me teach you, because I am humble and gentle, and you will find rest for your souls. For my yoke fits perfectly, and the burden I give you is light."

The Revelation:

Good morning my child and may my grace and peace be with you throughout this day. I want you to know you are welcome to come to me when you labor and are burdened. I can refresh and revive you. I would have you to know there are different ways you can come to me in this life. You can come to me in prayer. You can come to me by reading My Word. You can come to me through prayer and meditation. You can come to me through praise and worship. You can come to me through the Lord's Supper. When you draw near to me in any of these ways, I will draw near to you and I will enter into your soul and become one with you. I will become refreshment like food for your soul and grant you the strength to continue on your earthly journey. Many a persons have alienated themselves from me, especially in the times of weakness and weariness. I am here for you. You never have to journey alone nor suffer alone in this world. When you become tired, when you become lonely, when you become frustrated, don't run from me but run to me and I will comfort you. Don't let this life get the best of you. Come to me for rest and restoration and you will find peace for your soul. Nothing will happen in your life today that I can't handle.

The Response:

Gracious Lord, My God, I thank you for refreshing my soul through sleep last evening and I thank you just the same for waking me up to another blessed day. I pray that during this day when I become frustrated, burdened, and weary that I will come running to you for the refreshment of my spirit. Lord, I know you are a perfect friend and no one cares about my well being like you. I am thankful for the privilege of drawing near to you in fellowship of prayer and meditation. I am thankful for the privilege of being able to exchange the heavy burdens of this world for the burdens of Heaven. Thank you for receiving me when I am weary and anxious. Thank you for receiving me when I feel like I can't go on. Lord, I promise to turn and run to you when I need rest and relief. Amen.

Day 38

The Reading:

Hebrews 13:17, "Obey your spiritual leaders and do what they say. Their work is to watch over your souls, and they know they are accountable to God. Give them reason to do this joyfully and not with sorrow. That would certainly not be for your benefit."

The Revelation:

Good morning my child; may the grace and joy of Heaven shower down upon you today. Everyone must submit and be accountable to someone. All legitimate authority comes from me—the government, law enforcers, teachers, parents and spiritual leaders. When you obey those who have authority over you, you are obeying me. No one can decide what they will like or dislike. Why? Because your feelings are not always under control. Submission and obedience to those in legitimate authority is an act of the highest reasoning. Whenever you obey your leaders you are obeying me. Meditate upon this teaching and truth. Whenever you obey those over you it frees your mind from all sense of inferiority and diminishes the spirit of resentment that comes naturally. Obedience includes sacrifice. It means you are willing to sacrifice yourself, your time, your feelings, and your free will. The more you obey the purer your self-sacrifice becomes. Whenever you feel inclined to disobey, remember I lived a life of submission and sacrifice even unto the cross. Follow my example. Never, never be a bad example by disobedience. When you obey, it makes it easier for others to obey. When you try to live without obedience, you are putting yourself on a pedestal and that my child is pride and dangerous. No one can live without some form of obedience in this life. No one can be a good leader unless they themselves know how to obey. Obedience not only keeps your pride in check, it pleases my Father. Nothing will happen in your life today that I can't handle.

The Response:

O Lord, my God thank you for allowing me to see another day. Your love and mercy are unparallel. I am grateful for your guidance and direction through the Holy Spirit. As I submit to your Word, I want to be obedient and submit to those who are in authority over me. I know by submitting to them, I am submitting to you. I want to always obey you through them. I pray for the spirit of submission that I may please you and represent your presence in my life by being an example before others. Grant me the grace to hear your voice when I'm call to execute my daily duties. I desire to be totally committed and submitted to your Word and to those you have put in authority over me. Amen.

Day 39

The Reading:

Ephesians 6:12, "For we are not fighting against people made of flesh and blood, but against the evil rulers and authorities of the unseen world, against those mighty powers of darkness who rule this world, and against wicked spirits in the heavenly realms."

The Revelation:

Good morning my child and may the peace of My Father be yours in abundance today. Everyday your life will be engaged in spiritual warfare. There will be continual struggles going on around you and within you. The ultimate objective of these struggles is to win you over to Heaven or to win you over to Hell. The persons and parties involved in this spiritual struggle for your soul are the Holy Spirit and me versus the world, your flesh, and the Devil. The battleground for this warfare is your soul. Too often my children will fight against my help by joining their own enemies. They do this through foolish pride or through their blame-worthy ignorance. The world fights against me with its false standards of success and ambition. The flesh fights against me with its fleshly desires to satisfy its nature. The Devil takes advantage of these enemies and tempts you through your weaknesses. Your only defense against these notorious enemies is to become a spiritual person and fight against them every moment of every day like a good soldier. This battle for your soul and your salvation is a daily attempt to conquer you. You must never lose heart or yield to the seduction of sin under the Devil's disguises. If you continue to fight for my glory without self-consideration, you will become more than a conqueror. Nothing will happen in your life today that I can't handle.

The Response:

O Lord, my God, I am thankful and grateful for another day. Jesus, I yield to you as the Captain and commander of my soul. As I engage in daily warfare on this battlefield of life, I pray and ask you to lead me and guide me against the spiritual struggles for my soul. When I am tempted by the Devil, I pray for strength to resist him. When I am seduced by sins, I pray for strength to resist them. Help me to stand strong and firm as I seek to glorify your name in my daily battles and may my ability to remain steadfast be an inspiration to others as they, too, fight against sin and Satan. Amen.

Day 40

The Reading:

Romans 1:22-25, "Claiming to be wise, they became utter fools instead. And instead of worshiping the glorious, ever-living God, they worshiped idols made to look like mere people, or birds and animals and snakes. So God let them go ahead and do whatever shameful things their hearts desired. As a result, they did vile and degrading things with each other's bodies. Instead of believing what they knew was the truth about God, they deliberately chose to believe lies. So they worshiped the things God made but not the Creator himself, who is to be praised forever. Amen."

The Revelation:

Good morning my child; know that I am with you and will be by your side throughout this day. What is not God, is only a creature. Every person and every thing that is created in the world is a powerless creature. You should never prefer any of them over God. Nothing in this world can bring you perfect peace and joy, which can be your inheritance when you get to heaven. When your earthly journey comes to an end you will then realize how small and imperfect all the creatures you put your hopes in are compared to me and my Father. If your main concern and interests are in those things on earth then that's where you will put all of your energy and efforts. You will sin to attain what is earthly pleasurable; however, if you dedicate your interests to me, your desires for the earthly pleasures would be minimized. Your interests in me will be proven by your desire to please me daily and you will give me more of your time and attention. As long as any person or creature has the power to attract and draw you away from me, I am not your main interest. People and creatures may attract your attention and your feelings but they can never do for you what I can do for you. Strive to simplify and sanctify your daily life and divest yourself of useless and unnecessary interests. I am not saying it is wrong to love people or to desire the good things in life but when you desire them more than me I am not your Lord. Nothing will happen in your life today that I can't handle.

The Response:

Dear God, my gracious Savior, I am grateful for another day in this life. This is a perfect day to draw closer to you and glorify your name. Lord, I don't ever want to put any thing or anybody before you. You desire and deserve all that I am and have to offer. No one and no thing deserves my unconditional loyalty and love but you. Help me today to please you through my relationships or by abandoning whatever that attracts me from you. I sincerely desire to love you and please you above all things that are created. I pray that I will please you every hour of the day. No person or created thing shall ever usurp my love for you again. Amen.

Day 41

The Reading:

2 Kings 20:1, "About that time Hezekiah became deathly ill, and the prophet Isaiah son of Amoz went to visit him. He gave the king this message: "This is what the LORD says: Set your affairs in order, for you are going to die. You will not recover from this illness.""

The Revelation:

Good morning my child and welcome to this blessed day. Throughout this day meditate on the fact that your thoughts and actions should always be orderly governed with the expectation that you could die today. If you are not prepared to die today then how will you be prepared tomorrow? How do you know that you will even live to see tomorrow? If you have ever seen a person leave this world, take a moment and reflect upon the fact that you too shall leave this world. While yet you are healthy you could do many good deeds but when you become sick you will be very limited to what you can do. When a person has too many worldly interests they very seldom grow in holiness. They have too many distractions. Reflection and prayer are the seeds of a holy life and a holy life is the road to a holy death. The present time you have is precious, therefore, provide for yourself while you are still living. Do not depend on the prayers or provisions of others after you are dead. This is your day of preparation and salvation. Spend today productively. Keep sending up your prayers, your sacrifices, and your good deeds to me before you come to be judged by me. You have the opportunity and the time to gain eternal life by the wise use of your time. I pray that you will think of your death daily and know that lost time can never be recovered. Many people are dying at this moment who have wasted their time. If you don't prepare for death right now, today, you are not wise. Nothing will happen in your life today that I can't handle.

The Response:

Most gracious and forgiving Lord, I thank you for the blessing of this new day. I didn't earn it and I don't deserve it but I am grateful for having received it. As I live out this day grant me the mindset to meditate on the fact that death is closer to me than I can realize. Help me to live out this day pleasing you in thoughts, words, and desires. Help me to live this day preparing to meet death at any moment. I want to live a holy life in order to die a holy death. When my time comes to die, I pray that it will be nothing less than your loving voice calling me to come home. Amen.

Day 42

The Reading:

Proverbs 17:27-28, "A truly wise person uses few words; a person with understanding is even-tempered. Even fools are thought to be wise when they keep silent; when they keep their mouths shut, they seem intelligent."

The Revelation:

Good morning my child and welcome to another day that was ordained before the beginning of creation. There are times when you ought to keep to yourself and avoid any conversations. There is no merit in idle talk or indecent talk. Do not waste valuable time boasting or disputing with others. Always think before you speak and you will never regret your words. When a word has been spoken, it can never be recalled. Thoughtless talk is like an arrow loosely shot into a crowd. It will cause harm that is hard to undo. Try to be like many of the older saints who avoided the company of others when possible to stay closer to me. It has been wisely spoken, "As often as I have gone among men, I returned less a man." You, too, will come back less a man when you talk too much. It is easier to keep silent than it is to stop talking when you should. When you are silent and alone, I can speak to you without interruptions. You will hear my voice clearly through ideas, desires, and holy intentions. My child, learn to love silence and use it well. When you do, people will respect your judgment more. Each time you open your mouth let it be for a good and definite purpose and your wisdom will speak for itself. When you draw closer to me in silence, I will draw closer to you. Nothing will happen in your life to day that I can't handle.

The Response:

O Lord, my God how excellent and marvelous is thy name in all the earth. Thank you for waking me up this morning and blessing me with another opportunity to grow in the grace and knowledge of you. Throughout this day teach me how to listen more and talk less. It is my desire to avoid and shun idle and useless conversations. I only desire to speak to you and your mercy. In all of my conversations when I am compelled to speak grant that my words may never hurt anyone but bring consolation and inspiration to those in sorrow, guidance to those who are confused, light to those who are ignorant and hope to those who are in despair. Lord, take my lips and make them yours. I pray to become a man of silence and prefer only to talk to you. When I do speak let it be to bring people closer to you and you closer to them. May my words always be holy and acceptable to you. Amen.

The Reflection: [What I heard the Holy Spirit speaking into my spirit during the past seven days and how it changed me or challenged me].

Day 43

The Reading:

Matthew 19:20-22, ""I've obeyed all these commandments," the young man replied. "What else must I do?" Jesus told him, "If you want to be perfect, go and sell all you have and give the money to the poor, and you will have treasure in heaven. Then come, follow me." But when the young man heard this, he went sadly away because he had many possessions."

The Revelation:

Good morning my child and many blessings be unto you throughout this day. Listen to this; if you truly and sincerely desire to grow in perfection you must liberate your heart from all earthly attachments. The first thing is to break away from whatever attracts and draws you into sin. Then you will be able to engage in holy poverty. What is holy poverty? It is the desire and will to forsake more and more the materialistic things in your daily life in order to have fewer weights holding you back and down. I know it is impossible to abandon every thing in this life. I know that you must eat, work, rest and plan for your future. But when you satisfy your soul with a holy poverty, you are able to do all the other things in a perfect manner. In your holy poverty you will seek to use the materials of the world to please me and not allow them to hold you hostage in idolatry. Your holy poverty will make you wise in the right use of what you need. Please know that holy poverty of being poor does not mean having nothing. Again, it simply means you do not allow your soul to be so attached to the things that keep you from me. It simply means your desire to be in a right fellowship and friendship with me eliminates any and all competition within your soul. Nothing will happen in your life today that I can't handle.

The Response:

My Lord and my Joy, hallelujah to your name and thanks be unto you for another day on this side of eternity. Most gracious Lord, I desire to live this day striving to have fewer and fewer things of this world that may cause me to de distracted from you. I pray that you will fill my mind with nothing but thoughts of you and not the things of this world. In your word, you said,

'Blessed are the poor in spirit, for theirs is the kingdom of heaven.' Help me Lord to divest myself of any and all things that hinder a perfect relationship with you. Nothing in this world is important to me except pleasing you. Amen.

Day 44

The Reading:

Proverbs 16:18, "Pride goes before destruction, and haughtiness before a fall."

The Revelation:

Good morning my child; may you receive and enjoy this day with thanksgiving and peace in your heart. Whatever blessings you may have come your way never think more of yourself than you ought. Possess and honor me as your greatest blessing and let everything else take second place in your life. If you are popular, powerful, rich, or attractive always remember the truth about yourself and you will not become a victim of sinful pride. Stay humble. Whatever you possess, whatever is good and noble in you, it all belongs to me. Many people consider themselves better than their neighbors because of their talents, gifts, abilities, or status in life. All of these things come because of my favor. I could have easily given them to someone who is less gifted, less talented, and unknown. Yes, I want you to do as much good with the things you possess in this life but be very careful and cautious of becoming proud of yourself. Always know, you can do nothing without me. When you consider yourself better than others, you are thinking like a fool full of pride. James wrote in his letter, "God opposes the proud but gives grace to the humble." My child, always walk humble before your fellow man and you will find favor and grace with Me and My Father. Nothing will happen in your life today that I can't handle.

The Response:

Dear gracious Lord and Savior, I am blessed to receive this new day. Thank you for bringing me through another night into this day. Lord, I know who I am and what I am and what I possess all come from you. I am thankful for all the gifts and abilities you have endowed me with. I never want to think more of myself than I really am. I never want to lord myself over anybody as their superior. Grant me your grace to walk humbly before you and consider others more than me. Crucify the spirit of pride in me before it embarrasses me and ultimately destroys me. It is my desire to bless others with what I have and to glorify you in the name of Jesus. Amen.

Day 45

The Reading:

Proverbs 3:5-7, "Trust in the Lord with all your heart; do not depend on your own understanding. Seek his will in all you do, and he will direct your paths. Don't be impressed with your own wisdom. Instead, fear the Lord and turn your back on evil."

The Revelation:

Good morning my child; peace and blessings are yours today just for the asking. No one will ever be certain of their true self worth. It is only when you die will you ever know everything about yourself. As you live daily you will discover something about yourself that you did not know or even suspect the day before. Every person is a mystery even unto themselves. This is why it is easy to fall for your own self-deception. Your initial intentions may not be the real reason that motivates you. Deep within your subconscious there may be some selfish reasons behind your motives. Because of this teaching today, I do not want you to trust in your own intentions but develop a healthy and holy trust in me for daily counsel and guidance. It is dangerous to trust yourself too much no matter how holy you believe yourself to be. Lean not unto your own understanding alone, but call on me and count on me for wisdom and understanding. Without me you are nothing. Without me you can never do anything that will be worthy of Heaven. This lesson today is not meant to alarm you or to make you an abnormal self-centered person but to simply admonish you to live according to the truth. Just like the saints of old always be suspicious of self. A holy self-contempt and a holy self-distrust will keep you from taking any chances with your own self-deception. Keep your eyes on my perfection and practice daily self-denial and you will avoid deceiving yourself. Nothing will happen in your life today that I can't handle.

The Response:

Gracious, kind and tender loving Savior, I am thankful and blessed to behold another day of life. I desire to make you and keep you first in my life. I am willing, with your help, to control this blind self-seeking self within me. No matter how wise I am; no matter how holy I am, I am unmatched for your wisdom and understanding. Grant me the grace to practice more prayers, more self-denial, and more leaning on you for guidance and peace. Let me treat this foolish self within me with the contempt it deserves. I truly yearn to please you and yield to your will and your way everyday. Amen.

Day 46

The Reading:

Matthew 7:1-5 "Stop judging others, and you will not be judged. For others will treat you as you treat them. Whatever measure you use in judging others, it will be used to measure how you are judged. And why worry about a speck in your friend's eye when you have a log in your own? How can you think of saying, 'Let me help you get rid of that speck in your eye,' when you can't see past the log in your own eye? Hypocrite! First get rid of the log from your own eye; then perhaps you will see well enough to deal with the speck in your friend's eye."

The Revelation:

Good morning my child, and may you be encouraged and inspired by the Holy Spirit during the day. You must learn to be patient and understanding with the shortcomings of your neighbors. They are patient with your shortcomings. When you fail to correct your own faults how can you expect others to correct theirs? In your desire to see others change, you must be willing to fight just as hard to change and correct yourself. It is not fair for you to try and correct others; yet resent it when someone corrects you. It is not fair for you to demand others to play by the rules yet your anger is aroused when the rules are brought to your attention. In judging your neighbor, always use the same love and understanding that you use to judge yourself or desire others to use when judging you. You only delude and deceive yourself when you think your actions are pleasing to others when actually they are displeasing. One sure way of proving your love to me is by being patient with others as they wrestle with their faults. Just as you excuse yourself when you are at fault I desire you to treat your neighbor with that same love for their mistakes. And know that nothing will happen in your life today that I can't handle.

The Response:

Oh Lord, my God, thank you for watching over me last night and waking me up this morning. Teach me today how to think well and treat my neighbor with patience and understanding inspite of their faults. I pray that I will never displease you by my deliberate intolerance or harshness towards those around me. Remind me often of my own faults and limitations so that I may include myself when I pray for others. Lord, it is my daily desire to prove my love and gratefulness for you through my loving treatment of others. I love you Lord. Amen.

Day 47

The Reading:

Matthew 22:37-40, "Jesus replied," `You must love the Lord your God with all your heart, all your soul, and all your mind.' This is the first and greatest commandment. A second is equally important: `Love your neighbor as yourself.' All the other commandments and all the demands of the prophets are based on these two commandments."

The Revelation:

Good morning my child, and welcome to another ordained day. Your love for me is illustrated in your willingness to suffer and sacrifice yourself for me. When you disagree with my will, you are limiting your love for me. When your love is unconditional you are ready to endure anything in your daily life. Your eyes will be so fixed on me that you won't even notice who is causing you to suffer. When you truly love me with all of your heart, soul and mind, I become your motive, I become your strength and I become your only goal in life. When you love me with all of your heart, soul and mind you hold nothing back; you make no reservations for yourself and your only desire is to fully please me. It is a foolish thing to place any created thing before me or desire any created thing more than me. There should be no competition in your heart for your love towards me. When you have learned to love me in a degree that exceeds your love for any and every thing else, then your love for me will be complete. This is the kind of love worthy of my Father and my full love in return. When your love is complete and full for my Father and me, you will then know a peace and a joy beyond all understanding. Strive daily to love me this way and remember, nothing will happen in your life today that I can't handle.

The Response:

Most gracious, kind and all loving God, I am thankful and grateful for the gift of this new day. Thank you for keeping watch over me during the night Lord. Teach me how to love you and my neighbor as I love myself. Teach me how to imitate Christ and His perfect acts of love. I pray that my love for you and for my neighbor is worthy of Heaven. Throughout this day grant me more of your love, more of your grace and more of your wisdom that I may love and experience love for your sake. Use me as a role model of love that others may see and believe. Do with me as you wish only let me be worthy of gaining heaven. Amen.

Day 48

The Reading:

Psalm 37:1-4 "Don't worry about the wicked. Don't envy those who do wrong. For like grass, they soon fade away. Like springtime flowers, they soon wither. Trust in the Lord and do good. Then you will live safely in the land and prosper. Take delight in the Lord, and he will give you your heart's desires."

The Revelation:

Good morning my child, and may the blessings of Heaven be yours today. I desire you to seek your glory from me and me alone. Let others seek their worldly glory from one another if they wish. Their glory is only empty and without merit. True greatness and glory can never be attained through worldliness. My standards of greatness are not like the world standards. Your worth is not estimated by your knowledge or by your position in society or by your visions. Your true worth is gauged by your humility and love. Please do not think too much of yourself or desire the praises of others. Do not become envious or covet the honor and false glory people of the world receive; true honor and glory is found only in forgetting yourself to the point of being despised and humbled for my sake. Worldly honor is like the fading of a flower. It doesn't last long. People will soon forget. But when you delight yourself in me; when you trust only in my truths; I will esteem and exalt you before the world. Remember, the only lasting honor is my Father's approval. All other standards that disagree or conflict with His are false and foolish. Nothing will happen in your life today that I can't handle.

The Response:

Dear God, my glory and my honor—I praise you and I thank you for the beauty of this day. As I go about this day it is my desire to keep my mind and eyes on you and not the world. I pray that the spirit of covetousness for the things of this world does not distract my attention from following you. Help me to resist the seductions of this world. Help me to resist the false glory of the wicked and do not become envious of them. My desire is to trust only in you and your truth. My heart yearns only for your highest holiness and true glory. I pray for the grace to stay focus only on those things that move me closer to Heaven. Amen.

Day 49

The Reading:

Psalm 136:1-3, "Give thanks to the Lord, for he is good! His faithful love endures forever. Give thanks to the God of gods. His faithful love endures forever. Give thanks to the Lord of lords. His faithful love endures forever."

The Revelation:

Good morning my child, peace, blessings and joy be unto you as you live out this day. My child, never let gratitude and the spirit of thanksgiving leave your heart. I am always worthy of praise and thanksgiving. Think about it; who gives you each moment of life; who offers you mercy when you sin; who sends you grace to fight against and resist daily temptations? I do. And I do it all because I love you. My only desire is to raise you up in a heavenly glory. Your greatest ingratitude will be your ingratitude towards me. No one else on earth deserves the gratitude that you owe me. Your ingratitude will prevent me from blessing you with more favor and grace. When you are ungrateful you limit the full potential of the gifts I have given you. When you desire the gift more than you desire the Giver of the gift—you are prone to fall into sin. When you neglect to depend completely upon me—you begin to exalt yourself and that is pride. I want you to be a person of truth always and I mean always refuse to live a lie. Be grateful for what I have blessed you with. Never consider yourself worthy of anything or more than what you are. Remember without my grace you are nothing. Be thankful in all things, the pleasant as well as the difficult. Know that your life is in my hands and accept it with gratitude. Nothing will happen in your life today that I can't handle.

The Response:

My Lord, and My God, I am thankful and grateful for this new day. Thank you for keeping watch over me during the night. I want to thank you also for your grace and your mercy that are extended to me every day. Without you my being could not be possible. Each and every second of my life is a precious gift from you. I am forever grateful for all that you do in my life. And I will express my gratitude not only in words but how I live each day. Thank you shall always be my words of praise. Amen.

The Reflection: [What I heard the Holy Spirit speaking into my spirit during the past seven days and how it changed me or challenged me].

Day 50

The Reading:

Luke 6:26 "What sorrows await you who are praised by the crowds, for their ancestors also praised false prophets."

The Revelation:

Good morning my child, and I hope that you enjoyed sweet sleep and peace last evening. Today I want to teach you not to desire or be anxious to make a good impression to be esteemed by others. Many people have a strong need to be liked by many friends through at times it may be good to be esteemed, it can also be dangerous. This can make you more eager to please people than to please me. Yes, do your best to show a reasonable amount of respect and consideration to every one but never forget you owe me your highest honor. Always treasure my love and fellowship. I will always tell you the truth. Avoid anyone who draws you away from the truth or who applauds sin. It is also wise not to let your neighbor get to know you too well. Becoming too familiar or acquainted with anyone may reveal your faults and shortcomings, which may have never been suspected before. When this happens your neighbor may lose the inspiration, which your words had previously given. Never fear being a hypocrite; as long as you are striving to become as good as others think you are. You will find too often people will judge you more by your failures and faults than by your efforts and ideals. It is not wise to fix your heart on human favor and approval. What other people think of you will often depend on what they think of themselves. Human approval is not always the truth. Sometimes, it is best not to seek human attention and admiration and be content with seeking me in solitude. Human praise can cause your head to swell with pride. Only I know what you really are and will esteem you as you deserve. Nothing will happen in your life today that I can't handle.

The Response:

Most kind and loving God, I am thankful for the bonus of another day. It is truly a precious gift to be alive. Lord, teach me how to please you and only you. Let me not give too much credence to my neighbor's opinion of me, good or bad. Your approval is all that matters to me. I can never hope to please you and at the same time please everyone else. My desire today is to find favor with you and to follow your will in all things. I need not care for a single second what anyone may think or say. Only you really know me and love me. Amen.

Day 51

The Reading:

Ecclesiastes 2:10-11 "Anything I wanted, I took. I did not restrain myself from any joy. I even found great pleasure in hard work, an additional reward for all my labors. But as I looked at everything I had worked so hard to accomplish, it was all so meaningless. It was like chasing the wind. There was nothing really worthwhile anywhere."

The Revelation:

Good morning my child and welcome to another blessed filled day. Did you know vanity is another name for foolish expectation and useless pretense? Many people expect too much from the good things of this world and others pretend to be bigger than they really are. They try to attract more attention than they really deserve. Vanity of vanities, all is vanity for those who do not love me and seek me first. Vanity of vanities—all is vanity for those who do not follow my commandments. There is a absolutely nothing permanent under the sun. Whenever you love something for its own sake and not because it helps you to carry out my will, my child you are a victim of vanity. When death comes, all will be taken away and nothing left. This is the truth! It is vanity to strive excessively and impulsively for things that are perishing. It is vanity to be over eager for honors; it is vanity to consider yourself better than others; it is vanity, my child, to follow the desires of the flesh. These things will only bring a penalty later in life. Many are living and have died not knowing that vanity is wishing for a long life and not caring about living a holy life or giving their entire attention to the present and not thinking about eternity. It is all vanity to love what is passing away moment by moment instead of fixing your heart on Heaven, the home of endless joy. Trust me, if those who have died could relive their lives, their values would be different. Nothing will happen in your life today that I can't handle.

The Response:

O Lord my God and my Savior, I am grateful for your grace as I slept last night. Thank you for waking me up this morning to see another consecrated day. I ask that you grant me wisdom that I may learn to value those things that are eternal. I do not wish to exhaust a lot of energy and effort on things that are passing away. Help me to understand all things according to their purpose and importance. As I pursue Heaven and happiness, help me to avoid everything and anything that seeks to consume my time and attention and make my life difficult. Lord, I desire only you. Amen.

Day 52

The Reading:

Romans 5:20-21, "God's law was given so that all people could see how sinful they were. But as people sinned more and more, God's wonderful kindness became more abundant. So just as sin ruled over all people and brought them to death, now God's wonderful kindness rules instead, giving us right standing with God and resulting in eternal life through Jesus Christ our Lord."

The Revelation:

Good morning my child and may the blessings of Heaven engulf you throughout this day. There is nothing on this earth that can compare to my grace. My grace is richer, deeper, and more glorious than any and all possessions or achievements you can imagine. My grace shows you what is better and more profitable for your eternal success. My grace strengthens you to resist sinful attractions and keeps you focus on those things, which are holy. My grace brings a yearning for Heaven down within your soul. All graces are gifts and blessings from me. My grace cannot help you unless you accept it and use it according to my will. You must read, reflect, and pray so that you may gain understanding with what I want you to know. My grace contains three elements: 1) it enlightens the mind to know truth; 2) it inclines your will towards that which is holy and 3) it offers you strength to follow after righteousness. My grace is distributed equally to each individual according to his or her abilities and efforts. Sometimes I may speak words. Sometimes I may send an instant message via various venues and sometimes I may speak through your praying and reflecting and reading. It is because of my grace that you are able to understand what you read or hear in a sermon. Always know that I am ready to bless you with my grace every step of you daily life. Nothing will happen in your life today that I can't handle.

The Response:

Most gracious, kind and loving God, thank you for this day. This day is another opportunity to experience your grace and your mercy. I only ask for wisdom today to hear and listen to your voice as you speak to me. I am grateful for your grace and I do not want to ever take it for granted. It is my desire today to live as an example of your grace and to reflect your holiness all day. There is no greater gift one can receive than the gift of your grace. Thank you Lord for looking beyond my faults and granting me your grace. Amen.

Day 53

The Reading:

Romans 12:17-19, "Never pay back evil for evil to anyone. Do things in such a way that everyone can see you are honorable. Do your part to live in peace with everyone, as much as possible. Dear friends, never avenge yourselves. Leave that to God. For it is written, "I will take vengeance; I will repay those who deserve it," says the Lord."

The Revelation:

Good morning my child, and may the favor of Heaven be with you today. When it comes to anger anybody can get along with those who are easy going and mild tempered. It is no great thing to associate with people with whom you like or with those who agree with you. Your true greatness will be proven by getting along with people who are very difficult, negative and contrary to holiness. There are those who live at peace with themselves and other around them. There are others who have no personal peace within themselves and they are determined to ruin the peace of others. My child, you will only find peace if you are willing to be patient with that you cannot resolve. When you learn how to suffer patiently for my sake you will receive the gift and grace of my peace. When troubles and trials confront you do not become disturbed. If you cannot find a resolution on your own it means I want you to learn something from the situation. Trust in me always. Avoid anger at all cost when the situation does not favor you. Do not let any words of resentment fall from your lips. Set a good example of faith and always show confidence in my word. Never lose control and never return anyone evil for evil; always leave room for my wrath. Nothing will happen in your life today that I can't handle.

The Response:

Gracious Lord and merciful Father, I am thankful for this day and I will strive to live out it's hours pleasing you. As I go through this day grant me the patience to practice meekness and self-control. Help me to understand that meekness is not weakness, but inner strength and virtue. Do not let me give in to pride, which may lead to the sin of anger. When I feel wronged by others teach me not to return evil for evil but model the example of Jesus Christ with humility and self-control. I desire to please you and to represent your holiness at all times. Amen.

Day 54

The Reading:

Hebrews 9:27 "And just as it is destined that each person dies only once and after that comes judgment."

The Revelation:

Good morning my child and welcome to another day. A day that my love and blessings will sustain you. The time is coming when you will have to give account of your life on earth. Yes, you are going to stand before me and I will judge you. There will be no excuses accepted. There will be no bribes to buy me off. It is critically important that you take advantage of how you live your life now before it is over. Your sins can be forgiven now. You can repent of any wrong doing now. You can walk in holiness now. You can begin today preparing for the Day of Judgment. If you begin now living according to my commandments the Day of Judgment will not terrify you. On the Day of Judgment, no one will be able to speak for you or defend you. Each person will have to give an account for their own sins and answer for their own life. While you are alive and on earth, make every effort to purify your soul. You have every opportunity to seek my Father's forgiveness and correct any sinful habits before you die. When you put off repenting until later, you are playing a dangerous game with our soul. No one can repent after death. The only thing left after death is the judgment. It is imperative that you examine your life today and correct what needs to be corrected and then draw forever close to me through prayer, reading the word and daily fellowship. Nothing will happen in your life today that I can't handle.

The Response:

Oh Lord my God, thank you for blessing me with another day's journey. You brought me through another night and I am grateful. As I live this day I want to be in preparation for the soon coming judgment. I want to begin now confessing and repenting of any known sins. I want to begin now purifying my soul of any thing that may cause me to miss out on Heaven. Teach me during this day to confess the little sinful things now so that I may not suffer for them in the hereafter. Lord, I don't want to be judged and go to hell. I want to please you in this life so that I may enjoy eternity with you in the next life. Wash me thoroughly of any iniquity and prompt me to recognize any sins in my life to be repented of and confessed before the judgment. Amen.

Day 55

The Reading:

Luke 12:20-21 "But God said to him, `You fool! You will die this very night. Then who will get it all?' "Yes, a person is a fool to store up earthly wealth but not have a rich relationship with God."

The Revelation:

Good morning my child and blessings be unto you from all of Heaven. When your last day and hour arrive your view on life will be totally different. If your attitude towards my statues were nonchalant and careless; you will have great regrets. However, if you lived a life according to my word and my will your heart will be full of joy. Yes, the time is soon coming, when you will desperately desire another day or another hour to make amends of your past. Today is that day; the hour is that hour right now. No one can guarantee you another day or hour when you start slipping and ticking away. The spirit of death can come at anytime. You should always be prepared for it night and day. This way you will have nothing to fear no matter when the angels call and come for you. Live life in such a holy way that the appearance of death will bring you reckoned joy, and not regretful fear. Never, never love anything or anyone more than you love me. Invest all of your confidence in me and make me your greatest treasure. A weak soul is enslaved by the things of this world and its desires, but a prayerful soul gains heavenly liberty and the blessed assurance of seeing Heaven when death comes. Always live a prepared life anticipating the arrival of death. Very few people know that death is near. Nothing will happen in your life today that I can't handle.

The Response:

O' Lord, my God and my Saviour, thank you for blessing me to see another day and with another opportunity to draw closer to you. As I live out this day please make me wise in my preparation to meet death. I know death will come when I least expect it, but I don't have to be ill prepared to meet him. Lord, I don't want to do anything that will cause me to miss out on Heaven or separate me from your love. There is nothing or no one I desire more in this life than to be prepared to spend eternity with you. Teach me how to live each moment of the day getting ready for eternity. I am living to live again. Amen.

Day 56

The Reading:

Matthew 16:24 "Then Jesus said to the disciples, "If any of you wants to be my follower, you must put aside your selfish ambition, shoulder your cross, and follow me.""

The Revelation:

Good morning my child, welcome to another day created and ordained before the beginning of time. Always remind yourself that when I walked in this earthly life I had to endure many trials. As you remind yourself of this about me, never seek rest and pleasure for yourself on earth. It is not wise to expect anything other than suffering and persecution while you are still on the earth. Your life for my sake will be full of miseries and crosses to bear. Unfortunately, wherever you turn you will find a cross. If you bear your cross willingly, you will find greater strength in that cross and it will direct you towards the Kingdom of Heaven. On the other hand, if you resent your cross and bear it unwillingly, you will only make it a greater burden than it already is and you will still have to bear it. When you run away from one cross; you will find you are only running towards another cross, one that might be even heavier than the previous one. The only true and tried road to Heaven is by way of the cross. No one; you and no one else can escape the cross. Never fear your crosses. I am always near to help you to bear it and to endure it. When you embrace and endure your daily crosses for me, you are proving your love for me and your hunger for Heaven. Never resent your crosses or seek to avoid them. Remember not a single hour of my life was free of the cross and neither shall yours be. Follow my example in truth and in suffering and Heaven shall be yours. Nothing will happen in your life today that I can't handle.

The Response:

Greetings most merciful and gracious Lord, God. You are worthy of all honor and glory. I am eternally grateful for this blessing of another day. I desire and I'm determined to live it pleasing you. As I go about my daily duties keep me mindful of the cross. Your words speak loud and clear. If I love you, I'll love the cross and thus I am a true follower of yours. As I bear and endure my cross from day to day remind me that you are near me to help me to endure it. I am willing to submit to my daily cross, to deny myself and to follow you. Help me to recognize that the cross is my compass towards Heaven. Amen.

The Reflection: [What I heard the Holy Spirit speaking into my spirit during the past seven days and how it changed me or challenged me].

_____

_____

_____

_____

_____

_____

_____

_____

_____

_____

_____

_____

_____

_____

_____

_____

_____

_____

_____

_____

Day 57

The Reading:

Proverbs 18:24 "There are "friends" who destroy each other, but a real friend sticks closer than a brother."

The Revelation:

Good morning my child; blessings and peace are yours for the asking today. Everyone must have at least one friend in whom they can put their trust and confidence. Without a true friend you will never know or experience divine happiness. The more your friend means to you the greater your happiness will be. You will never find any human friend that will mean as much to you than I do. When you meditate on how much you mean to me and how much I've done for you it is then you will realize that I and I alone am your truest and closet friend. When you neglect my friendship and fellowship, you are neglecting the one you not only need the most but the one who loves you the most. Human friends can and will fail you by their inability to help you in the time of need. Even when they mean well they can inadvertently lead you astray. In me, you will have perfect and unfailing friendship. I am your forever friend. Always put your highest trust and confidence in me. I will never leave you; I will never forsake you. I will stick and stand by you even more so than your nearest relative. I am your friend. I laid down my life for you and none other can claim such an act for his or her friend. I am here for you. Call on me and count on me at all times. Nothing will happen in your life today that I can't handle.

The Response:

My God and my Redeemer, thank you for waking me up this morning. You have blessed me with another consecrated day and I am grateful. Not only that Lord, but also you are a true friend. You have always stood by my side; even when I've taking our relationship for granted, you have remained steadfast and not forsaken me. I realize more than ever now, no one can wish for any greater friend than you. I pray that I will never again waver in my trust in you as my friend and that I will never betray our friendship by sinning against you. Yes, I have human friends but none of them can compare to you and your love and loyalty for me. Thank you for being my friend and grant me the grace to forever embrace our friendship daily. I love you Lord. Amen.

Day 58

The Reading:

Deuteronomy 6:4-6, "Hear, O Israel! The Lord is our God, the Lord alone. And you must love the Lord your God with all your heart, all your soul, and all your strength. And you must commit yourselves wholeheartedly to these commands I am giving you today."

The Revelation:

Good morning my child and welcome to this day ordained and blessed for you as a gift from my Father. How great you become in this life will depend upon how much you love me. Your love for me must inspire you to want nothing but the best; to work for nothing but the best and to live for nothing but the best. As your Lord, I am the best. Compared to me everything on earth is fading away even as we speak now. When your desire and love for the best is center on me, you will be raised above yourself and above the temporal things in this life. Never let anything in this life turn your thoughts and desires from Me. Even when you are confronted with all kinds of suffering and trials in soul and in body, remain steadfast and continue to pursue my will. My grace will always be available for you when you are suffering for my sake. Your suffering is transforming you and sharpening your mind in order that you may see ever more clearly the highest and the holiest value of your daily walk with me. You will gain perfect strength so that no temptation or adversity can draw you away from my will or me. As your love for me grow and grow and grow, your self-interest will fade. When self is forgotten and your love for me is purified, you will live above all that is worldly and sinfully attractive. When you love me, you will know a peace others don't even suspect exist. When you love me with your all, yours will be happiness unknown to the earthly minded. Nothing will happen in your life today that I can't handle.

The Response:

Most excellent, gracious, and all loving God, I greet you in a spirit of gratitude and love for granting me the gift of another blessed day. My greatest glory on earth is to submit and surrender my allegiance to you today. I desire to love you with a purified and perfect love. I yield to whatever it takes to bring my love to an unconditional level that I may love you with all my mind, heart and soul. Let everything that I have ever placed above you decrease today and you increase in my life. Grant me the privilege of being in your hands, directed by your thoughts and your will. May my love for you be great and true. Amen.

Day 59

The Reading:

Proverbs 4:1-4, "My children, listen to me. Listen to your father's instruction. Pay attention and grow wise, for I am giving you good guidance. Don't turn away from my teaching. For I, too, was once my father's son, tenderly loved by my mother as an only child. My father told me, "Take my words to heart. Follow my instructions and you will live."

The Revelation:

Good morning my child and know that you are blessed and favored today. When you learn to listen and hear only my voice you will make great progress in little or no time. When you listen and obey my voice you will gain much, much more than anyone who relies only on his or her abilities and talents. My holy lessons bring wisdom, peace, and spiritual strength. As my faithful student of the cross you must learn to value earthly things for what they are really worth. Earthly things quickly fade away. Earthly values and prosperity are short lived. Only the joys of Heaven last forever. Each of my lessons is tailored and suited to each individual believer; I use different and various means to reach each soul. Whether it is through books, songs, prayers or quiet meditation, I give them light to understand and discern higher and holy wisdom. What I teach each individual depends on his or her personal spiritual level. Some will never get beyond the most basic knowledge of the faith because they never make any effort to rise higher. When you strive to draw and grow closer to me, I grant greater understanding and wisdom of the truth. When you listen and obey my teachings, I graciously grant a deep insight into spiritual things. As you grow in holy wisdom beware of foolish extremes, these acts are never inspired by me, they are the results of spiritual pride and gluttony. A true student of the Word always trusts in my voice. Nothing will happen in your life today that I can't handle.

The Response:

O God, my God thank you for allowing me to witness the dawning of another day. It is my desire to live it holy and acceptable unto you. As I go about my duties today, I pray that I will stay tuned in to your voice and your teachings.

I am eager to grow in the grace and knowledge and the wisdom of your word. Infuse me today with divine insight that I might move a little higher and a little closer to Heaven. Make me deaf to the voices of this world so I may hear only you. I pray to become an active listener who follows faithfully what you teach. Speak to me Lord; I am listening. Amen.

Day 60

The Reading:

Matthew 6:5-6, "And now about prayer. When you pray, don't be like the hypocrites who love to pray publicly on street corners and in the synagogues where everyone can see them. I assure you, that is all the reward they will ever get. But when you pray, go away by yourself, shut the door behind you, and pray to your Father secretly. Then your Father, who knows all secrets, will reward you."

The Revelation:

Good morning my child and welcome to this blessed and appointed day. Think about this, whenever people march in a parade they all keep the same step and pace. They march in one single formation with each other. When the parade is over, you notice each person walks in his own way and at his own pace. No two persons will walk the same or at the same pace. The same is true with prayer, when in public you all pray a public prayer at the same pace and with the same tone of voice; but in private you pray differently. You have your own special way of expressing yourself to me. Some will pray with prayer books; some will pray using the Bible, some will pray out of deep imagination picturing me with them in conversation. There are those who like to pray for sinners and there are those who simply like to kneel in my presence and enjoy my closeness. In any way, prayer is raising your thoughts and consciousness and your will to me. In prayer you stand before me in respect and with gratitude. Some will find it a challenge to attain this discipline with me. But you are to be a prayerful person, seeking my will and my grace daily for your journey. Through your prayers always seek to unite your mind and will with mine. I love you so much and desire to hear you talk to me daily. The more you talk to me, the more you will come to know me; the more you know me, the more you will love me. Nothing will happen in your life today that I can't handle.

The Response:

Most holy and loving God, I am indeed grateful for another day. As always you have kept me and sustained me. I am truly thankful. Now Lord, teach me how to pray. It is my desire to talk to you daily; all through the day. I want to know you more so I can love you more. It is a must that I pray and pray earnestly to you. Without prayer I know I only become less of a person. So, teach me like you taught your disciples how to pray. Grant me the grace to draw closer to you in prayer today and abide in your presence for fellowship and strength. Help me and hear my prayer. Amen.

Day 61

The Reading:

Mark 1:35, "The next morning Jesus awoke long before daybreak and went out alone into the wilderness to pray."

The Revelation:

Good morning my child and I pray that you found sweet sleep and peace to be yours last evening. Today, I want to teach you a great value in praying in solitude. When you talk to me in prayer you often find yourself distracted or coming away feeling empty or with unwanted desires. Whenever you communicate with me through prayer your understanding and faith should deepen and broaden. Yes, unlike human conversations, which only bring about a false esteem for the passing glories of this earth, praying to me brings and enlightens you with a clearer vision of those things, which are eternal and everlasting. I want you to start drawing aside daily and resting in my company. Learn to appreciate my fellowship and friendship in secret solitude. This will help you to keep a holy desire for the things of Heaven, a clear and undisturbed conscience and give you peace of mind. Learn to love to pray and labor unseen by humans and you will discover many, many ways of pleasing me more. You will discover my holy light will fall on your praying heart like seeds falling on rich and cultivated soil. You will soon discover it is easier to control your thoughts and desires by staying at home than by going out too often. Your coming and going out offer too many distractions and you lose focus of the faith. You cannot safely stand secure in public until you learn to grow steadfast in solitude. Even I had to withdraw in solitude to stay close to my Father. By this I was empowered and enabled to execute my ministry. You, too, in prayerful solitude will learn to receive such power and a deep appreciation for being alone with me. Develop a strong desire and a daily discipline to steal away to be alone with me and you will find strength to live holy and successful on earth. Nothing will happen in your life today that I can't handle.

The Response:

Greetings most gracious and holy God; thanks be unto you for waking me up to another glorious day. Thanks be unto you for attracting my mind to be in fellowship with you today. I pray that throughout this day I will seek to get alone with you to share moments of quiet and secret solitude. I strongly desire to grow in my consciousness of you and to become more like you. I pray that I will learn to turn to you as easily as I turn to my family and friends. Lord, I desire to be with you throughout this day. Help me to develop a stronger prayer life through solitude with you. Before I begin each day in public move and motivate me to begin each day in private prayer. Amen.

Day 62

The Reading:

2 Timothy 4:6-8, "As for me, my life has already been poured out as an offering to God. The time of my death is near. I have fought a good fight, I have finished the race, and I have remained faithful. And now the prize awaits me—the crown of righteousness that the Lord, the righteous Judge, will give me on that great day of his return. And the prize is not just for me but for all who eagerly look forward to his glorious return."

The Revelation:

Good morning my child and welcome to another day designed for you by Heaven. At the moment, you may not understand this, but it is designed by Heaven that you experience on earth times of trial and trouble. When pains, problems, and persecutions come your way it is done for your own good. They simply are sent to help you grow closer to me. You are to expect to encounter more trials and cross bearing than rest and daily pleasures. Peace and holiness will not come as quickly as you desire. Thus, you must be prepared to exercise patience rather than enjoy comfort. Do not be like some who are more interested in enjoying my gifts than earning my gifts. No, if you want to gain Heaven you must do things my way and submit to my will daily. In your times of trial wait for my strength which I will send in due time. Never give up the fight against your faults and frailties but exercise the courage and the patience to become the person of holiness that I would have you to become. Always keep the faith no matter what the circumstance and you will be rewarded accordingly when the time comes. Yes, Heaven is your reward and a crown is waiting on you. Your honest daily efforts against sin and your daily faithful attempt to please my Father will bring you closer and closer to being crowned. Keep fighting, keep the faith, and finish the course assigned to you. Nothing will happen in your life today that I can't handle.

The Response:

Most gracious and ever caring God thank you for watching over me during the night and for waking me up this morning. I am grateful for your grace. As I live out this day, help me to see your holy and guiding hands in all that

I am to go through today. Grant me the grace and the strength to fight the good fight of faith no matter what the test or trial. Lord, help me to run and finish the course laid out before me. I know Heaven is more than I will ever deserve and the crown that is stored up for me I will never be truly worthy of but at least I can do me best to please you and hope in you each day for the victory. Amen.

Day 63

The Reading:

1 Samuel 15:22-23, "But Samuel replied, "What is more pleasing to the Lord: your burnt offerings and sacrifices or your obedience to his voice? Obedience is far better than sacrifice. Listening to him is much better than offering the fat of rams. Rebellion is as bad as the sin of witchcraft, and stubbornness is as bad as worshiping idols. So because you have rejected the word of the Lord, he has rejected you from being king.""

The Revelation:

Good morning my child; this is another day blessed and ordained by my Father. Enjoy it and use it to glorify Him and honor me. I know all things and see all things because I made all things and I am the reason they remain in existence. Whatever exists or has power or ahs abilities is all because of me. Whatever happens or does not happen is foreseen, planned, and permitted by me. I know the plans I have for you. I seek your highest welfare, a welfare that is true, solid, and lasting. When you feel like second guessing my wisdom or motives, remember you are finite and I am infinite. When you disagree with my plans you are not only negating your own future, you are questioning my sovereignty. When I decide something differently from you it is because your choice is not for your best interest. I implore you to do what you think best but whenever necessary seek my counsel and be willing to obediently accept my decision. Punctuate every petition made before me with this perfect ending, 'Lord, if this is really good for me, please let it be; if not let your perfect will be done.' My child, place your hopes at my feet and leave the rest to me. Whatever you do always obey my voice and submit to my will. Always rely on my wisdom and I will bring peace into your heart. I love you! Nothing will happen in your life today that I can't handle.

The Response:

Dear Lord, my God and my guide, I am truly grateful for another day's journey. I could have died in my sleep but you kept me. I am thankful. As I live out this day, it is my desire to submit unto your perfect will and to obey your voice in all things. Please grant me the wisdom and the willingness to prefer your will and your way to my own. The worst harm that can come to me is my own disagreement with your loving and divine plan for my life. I here and now submit and place my life at your feet. Have your own way with me today and everyday. I shall not rebel or complain against you. Dear Lord, now I know there is no other way than to trust and obey. Amen.

The Reflection: [What I heard the Holy Spirit speaking into my spirit during the past seven days and how it changed me or challenged me].

_____

_____

_____

_____

_____

_____

_____

_____

_____

_____

_____

_____

_____

_____

_____

_____

Day 64

The Reading:

Matthew 25:14-18, "Again, the Kingdom of Heaven can be illustrated by the story of a man going on a trip. He called together his servants and gave them money to invest for him while he was gone. He gave five bags of gold to one, two bags of gold to another, and one bag of gold to the last—dividing it in proportion to their abilities—and then left on his trip. The servant who received the five bags of gold began immediately to invest the money and soon doubled it. The servant with two bags of gold also went right to work and doubled the money. But the servant who received the one bag of gold dug a hole in the ground and hid the master's money for safekeeping."

The Revelation:

Good morning my child; I pray that you will embrace my grace and walk in my anointing today. As I told my first disciples, I also tell you, as the Father has loved me, I also love you. All people receive life and being and strength from me, whether they are great or small, rich or poor, gifted or not gifted. I am the fountain of all-good. I know what each individual needs on a daily basis and only I decide how much each shall receive. The one who may receive little doesn't need to become jealous or envy of the one who may receive much. If you would keep your eyes focused on me and put your life totally in my hands you will find it easy to be content with what you have been blessed with. My love for you is more than any tangible gift that you can receive. Even your trials and troubles are as much a gift from me than peace and consolation. Why? Because they help shape your character and confidence in me. Too often my saints see only natural gifts and they fail to look beyond the natural and see my loving presence and hand guiding them. Always remember, it is I who bless you with what you have and I know what you can and cannot handle. Use what you have to honor me and your reward will be rich in Heaven. Nothing will happen in your life today that I cannot handle.

The Response:

Gracious God and keeper of my soul; Oh how thankful I am for your grace and kindness to permit me to see another day. I'm thankful for not only this day but for the gifts and graces you have endowed me with to honor and glorify you with throughout the day. I pray that I won't take for granted my gifts nor neglect to use them in your honor. I know someday I will have to give an account for what I do and don't do with these gifts from Heaven. So, teach me how to use them to advance your purpose and plan on this planet. I need not be jealous of what others have but only be grateful for what I have. I am thankful for my gifts and seek to let you govern my life through them. Amen.

Day 65

The Reading:

1 Corinthians 1:17-18, "For Christ didn't send me to baptize, but to preach the Good News—and not with clever speeches and high-sounding ideas, for fear that the cross of Christ would lose its power. I know very well how foolish the message of the cross sounds to those who are on the road to destruction. But we who are being saved recognize this message as the very power of God."

The Revelation:

Good morning my child and may you receive the peace and grace that are yours for the asking today. When you fully come to understand the value and the victory of the cross, you will no longer shun it or avoid it. You will willingly embrace the cross with great joy. In the cross, you will come to know and experience true joy and deep peace. There are many who hate and fear the cross. Pray for them. It is by way of the cross you will gain a clear mind and see the value of what you are going through because of the cross. The cross will help you to think straight. The cross will help you to draw closer to me. The cross will free you from confusion, fear, and discontent. The cross is your signpost that leads you to Heaven. Not even temptations can shake the power of the cross for those who truly love it. There is absolutely nothing on earth better than the cross. More than anything else, the cross will enrich your soul and keep you humble. And yes, the cross will prepare you for your last and most important eternal evaluation. That's why I commanded; 'If anyone wishes to come after me, let him deny himself, take up his cross, and follow Me.' How you handle and embrace the cross will determine where you spend eternity. Never forget this truth, through many trials you will enter into my kingdom, take up your cross daily and follow me. Nothing will happen in your life today that I can't handle.

The Response:

Oh Lord, my God and my example, I receive this day as a bonus from eternity. As I begin and live out this day, I pray that I will embrace and bear my cross as my Savior did. I accept my daily cross and yield to its power to keep me humble and devoid of pride. I accept my daily cross from your hands. I embrace it as a privilege and willingly and gladly bear it for the rest of my life. I now pray and ask for strength to press on when feelings within my flesh suggest that I forsake and deny the cross. Help me to live and bear my cross as Christ did. He died for me to prove His love for me. I shall bear my cross to prove my love for Him. Thank you for the cross. Amen.

Day 66

The Reading:

1 Corinthians 13:13, "There are three things that will endure—faith, hope, and love—and the greatest of these is love."

The Revelation:

Good morning my child; I pray that you will receive this day as an ordained gift from Heaven. I want you to know and understand this day that love is the greatest virtue of them all. Love is the energy that attracts people to me and makes them resemble me the most. Love is the virtue that makes you devoted, sincere, patient, longsuffering, forgiving, and strong. Wherever love reigns there will always be peace, and generosity. Love desires only one thing and that is to please the loved one. Your love for me will make you also humble, honest, obedient and unselfish. When your love is pure and sincere for me, you will always be willing to suffer anything for my sake. You will carry your burdens without feeling the weight of the load. You will seek to do more and not less. You will never complain or think about giving up. You will be willing to try anything even that which may seems impossible. When the spirit of true, agape love fills your heart you will constantly be on the look out to do more for me. Your love for me will give you joy when you feel fatigue and will motivate you to keep on keeping on. There is absolutely nothing stronger, nothing higher, nothing deeper, nothing more complete, nothing in Heaven or on earth that is greater than love. Your love for your neighbor will model your love for me. People will experience my love and who I am through you. Let your love be perfect. Nothing will happen in your life today that I can't handle.

The Response:

Most gracious Lord God, I am wonderfully and eternally grateful for this new day as I live this day according to your will, teach me how to love you and represent your love in all things. Because you are love and you first loved me, I want to please you and find favor with you by living out that love by showing it to others. Grant me more of your grace to love like you love. As I journey throughout this day, help me to abandon my selfish desires and do only what will please you. I know I can't lose with love. Jesus loved me and now helps me to love others in that same way. Grant that my love may be a light that attracts others to Christ and the cross. Amen.

Day 67

The Reading:

James 5:7-8, "Dear brothers and sisters, you must be patient as you wait for the Lord's return. Consider the farmers who eagerly look for the rains in the fall and in the spring. They patiently wait for the precious harvest to ripen. You, too, must be patient. And take courage, for the coming of the Lord is near."

The Revelation:

Good morning my child and may the blessings and peace of Heaven be yours today. I want to remind you that I came down from Heaven for your salvation and spiritual perfection. Not only did I make atonement for your sins but I also gave you an example of the virtue of patience. I suffered daily for your difficulties and trials in order to teach you and show you how to deal with them yourself. I had to practice a great deal of patience with all kinds of people in order to perfect that virtue. I had to endure the same kinds of people and personalities that daily annoy and irritate you. I desire you to learn from my patience and pray for the wisdom and endurance to imitate me. Yes, you are right, this life is full of demands and trials; contempt and hatred, and endless labors all of which demand great patience. Know this; by your unwavering patience you will earn a crown of unending glory. There are some who are only willing to suffer only what they choose to endure. There are some who will be patient with only certain people. But you are to be patient with everyone. Make no exceptions and set no conditions as to when and with whom you will be patient. When your patience is without prejudice, you seek to please me by accepting the trial as if my own hands handed them to you. A true person of patience does not see the people involved. That person only sees me and is willing to suffer and endure anything for my sake. Let this spirit be in you, be patient with everyone through everything. Nothing will happen in your life today that I can't handle.

The Response:

God of mercy, God of patience, I am grateful for this, another day on this side of Heaven. It is my desire to live it honoring and glorifying you. As I receive this day and am confronted by the many trials and challenges that may come my way, I pray that I will remember the patience of Christ and practice that same kind of patience. Help me to receive my sufferings as exercise that come to strengthen my ability to be patient and humble. I want to please you and be considered worthy of my heavenly crown. Grant me the grace to be gracious and patience with those who may seek to annoy and irritate me throughout this day (for your sake). I pray to be patience with others as you have been patience with me. Amen.

Day 68

The Reading:

James 1:22-25, "And remember, it is a message to obey, not just to listen to. If you don't obey, you are only fooling yourself. For if you just listen and don't obey, it is like looking at your face in a mirror but doing nothing to improve your appearance. You see yourself, walk away, and forget what you look like. But if you keep looking steadily into God's perfect law—the law that sets you free—and if you do what it says and don't forget what you heard, then God will bless you for doing it."

The Revelation:

Good morning my child; welcome to another day ordained before the beginning by my Heavenly Father. The lesson for today is to teach you not to be too impressed with people who can articulate the language beautifully. The standards of Heaven are not about words but action. The teachings from my word are meant to influence your will as you live out your daily life. Only through your action can you satisfy my heart. The most beautiful words in any earthly language are not half so beautiful and satisfying to me as a life of the one who follows my teachings daily. Please never spend time reading or learning anything for the sake of just appearing wise. Study and grow in knowledge only to improve your daily life. There are many who study to impress others. Their knowledge become vanity and idolatry because it does not make them better people or motivated to action. A good tree is known by its good fruit. A good person is known by doing good through thoughts, words and deeds. Yes, the desires of one's heart please me but I am only convinced by action. Never forget my words, 'If you love me keep my commandments and only the one who does the will of my Father will enter into Heaven.' Your daily actions are convincing proof that you really love me. Don't just be a hearer and a pontificator but be a doer of my word. Nothing will happen in your life today that I can't handle.

The Response:

My God and my Savior, thank you dearly for watching over me as I slept through the night and for waking me this morning to another beautiful day. Throughout this day I only seek to do your will. I desire to live out your commandments as a true disciple. I don't want to be just a hearer but a doer of your word. I pray that my life will reflect all that Jesus taught us in the Gospels. I pray that I will grow to become less and less a person of words and more and more a person of action. May my daily actions prove my loving loyalty to you from this day forward. Amen.

Day 69

The Reading:

Philippians 4:8-9, "And now, dear brothers and sisters, let me say one more thing as I close this letter. Fix your thoughts on what is true and honorable and right. Think about things that are pure and lovely and admirable. Think about things that are excellent and worthy of praise. Keep putting into practice all you learned from me and heard from me and saw me doing, and the God of peace will be with you."

The Revelation:

Good morning my child and may the blessings and favor of Heaven be yours for the asking. I've notice often times you kneel before me only in body. In spirit your mind is somewhere else and on something or someone else. I've noticed, too, that when you begin to meditate you start out thinking of me and talking to me but then you begin to drift mentally. In other words, you are spiritually distracted from your quality time with me. Let me show you where these distractions come from and how you can deal with them in order to remain loyal to our communion. Most distractions are thoughts, imaginations, feelings, and inward desires that arrest your attention undeservingly. When you should be focused and fixed on our fellowship you often find yourself fighting to keep control of your thoughts. These distractions are due to the various thoughts, images and experiences you allow yourself to become expose to on a daily basis. By eliminating and lessening these thoughts, images and experiences you will forbid and resist them from entering your mind. In order to stay focus on our relationship and beware of my forever nearness to you throughout the day, you must begin at once to examine and expel anything that may come between us and distract you spiritually. My child, unless you are determined to think and concentrate on that which is holy you will always find yourself victimized by daily distractions. Stay spiritually focused. Nothing will happen in your life today that I can't handle.

The Response:

Most glorious and honored Lord God, I thank you for another day in this life; a day to not only grow in grace but one to worship and glorify you. As I live out this day, I pray for your assistance to remain focus on those things, which are holy and noble. I pray that my mind will not wander from the truth of your word. I want to live this day fully devoted and attentive to your teachings and voice. Teach me how to control my thoughts when I am in prayer. There is nothing more valuable than our fellowship. It is my desire not to become distracted by the things of this world. Help me to guard against negative words, thoughts and images that try to enter my mind. Amen.

Day 70

The Reading:

Galatians 5:16-17, "So I advise you to live according to your new life in the Holy Spirit. Then you won't be doing what your sinful nature craves. The old sinful nature loves to do evil, which is just opposite from what the Holy Spirit wants. And the Spirit gives us desires that are opposite from what the sinful nature desires. These two forces are constantly fighting each other, and your choices are never free from this conflict."

The Revelation:

Good morning my child and blessed greetings from all of Heaven. If you really want to be a true follower of mine, you must learn to gain control of your natural desires and blind selfishness. The reason so many never enjoy fellowship with me is because they never submit to me completely. They give in to their fleshly desires and human appetites. Your flesh will always desire more than what is necessary. In order for you to gain control over your flesh you must intentionally and deliberately rid yourself of all unnecessary desires. You must learn to live with less and then you will have more room and more time for me. The more you surrender to your flesh the more you will be seduced away from me. The secret of a right fellowship with me lies in you separating yourself from as much of the things of this world as possible. You must turn your back and refuse all those things that threaten our relationship. Yes, you must even abandon any person or anything that does not aid and assist you in becoming a better person. Your life is too short; please don't waste it trying to gratify and satisfy the flesh. The flesh will never be satisfied. It is greedy. If you will put forth the daily effort in subduing your fleshly desires, I will help you to overcome those temptations. My grace will give you the desire to rise above your selfishness and seek my will. You will then learn to prefer my will and the world will become less important to you. Thus the foolishness of the flesh will not be appealing to you. Nothing will happen in your life today that I can't handle.

The Response:

O Lord my God and my redeemer, how grateful I am for your grace and your mercy. Morning by morning your grace is evident. Thank you for another day.

As I live out this day, teach me how not to yield to the desires of my flesh nor become blinded by my human appetites. Help me to be brave enough and strong enough to abandon anything and anybody that may lead me away from you. You and only you know what is good for me. I pray that I will submit and follow your spirit in everything I do throughout this day. I beg you for the strength and the power to follow your will when I am conflicted in the flesh. Let me yearn and burn for nobody and nothing but your will and your way. Amen.

The Reflection: [What I heard the Holy Spirit speaking into my spirit during the past seven days and how it changed me or challenged me].

Day 71

The Reading:

Galatians 3:1-3, "Oh, foolish Galatians! What magician has cast an evil spell on you? For you used to see the meaning of Jesus Christ's death as clearly as though I had shown you a signboard with a picture of Christ dying on the cross. Let me ask you this one question: Did you receive the Holy Spirit by keeping the law? Of course not, for the Holy Spirit came upon you only after you believed the message you heard about Christ. Have you lost your senses? After starting your Christian lives in the Spirit, why are you now trying to become perfect by your own human effort?"

The Revelation:

Good morning my child and welcome to another blessed filled day. There are many in the faith who are so easily tempted to disbelieve what my Word teaches. They have yet to realize the Devil is the enemy of truth. The Devil comes along to disturb their faith because he hates and fears a holy way of life in others. He does not spend a lot of time and energy on habitual sinners because he ensnares them through other means and sins. The Devil is a master at inspiring wrong doctrine among those in the church who are gullible and without a solid faith. He is able to disguise the error of his ways under the cloak of that which looks good. If you will stay close to me in fellowship and study you will not fall for his traps. The Holy Spirit will always lead you in the pathway of truth. Guard your mind with this truth and doubts from the Devil will not be able to rob you of your peace nor sway you from the faith. When you put and keep your trust in my word, the enemy will be put to flight. Continue to submit to the authority of my word and you will not be tricked by the Devil. All I ask of you is to live a virtuous life and maintain a strong faith. When you are obedient in this way, I will add more knowledge to your soul and nothing will be able to shake your faith. Nothing will happen in your life today that I can't handle.

The Response:

Oh Lord, my God and my Father, thank you for sparing my life once again to see and live another day. I pray that I will honor and glorify your name throughout this day. There are many things in this world I do not understand or can explain. But one thing I do know and believe and that is your word is the truth. I pray that I will stay in your word and depend on your word for revelation. My human ability to reason is too weak and too limited to grasp everything that happens in my life daily. I ask for discernment to resist the tricks and the traps of the Devil that seek to bewitch me. As I read and study your word, infuse me with wisdom, knowledge and understanding to remain steadfast in the faith. There is no other word; there is no other way but in Jesus Christ. Amen.

Day 72

The Reading:

Luke 22:41-42, "He walked away, about a stone's throw, and knelt down and prayed, 'Father, if you are willing, please take this cup of suffering away from me. Yet I want your will, not mine.'"

The Revelation:

Good morning my child; blessings and favor be unto you as you live out this day. Very few of my followers have perfect peace within their souls and it is all because they refuse to surrender their will to me and permit me to manage their lives. Too many of them put more faith in their limited abilities than they are willing to put in my infinite power. Yes, there are those who say they resign to my will but they do it with a few exceptions and with these exceptions they are willing to trust themselves rather than trust me. In these exceptions they are ready to sin rather than submit to change. Then there are others who do surrender their will to me but only for a season. After a while they become weak and impatient and reclaim their will. None of these souls will ever know me completely or intimately. Why? Because they refuse to yield to my perfect will and thus they forfeit the peace that could be theirs. My word to you on this day is to forget about self and let me guide and govern your life every day according to my will. Nothing you can offer me will please me until you have granted me the perfect gift of all that is your will. When you prefer and submit to whatever I send your way daily you are granting me your will. In everything that comes to you today seek out my will in it. When you are confronted and conflicted by matters that displease your spirit, seek out my will in them. When you imitate my ways in your life you are echoing "ot my will but your will be done." Remember nothing will happen in your life today that I can't handle.

The Response:

My Lord and my God, how excellent is your name in all the earth. I rise this morning with complete thanksgiving in my heart. You have blessed me with another day and I am thankful. I am beginning this blessed day by yielding to your holy will for my life. Even though I don't understand it all, I know your will is perfect. I pray that you will guide and govern my life today as I go about my divine duties and that my life will be a reflection of your holiness in thought and speech. On this day, I want to go on record saying I yield my will totally to you and I submit unconditionally to your authority. It is my daily desire to please you and find favor with you in this life as I strive towards Heaven. Hear I am; have your own way with me. Amen.

Day 73

The Reading:

Philippians 2:3-5, "Don't be selfish; don't live to make a good impression on others. Be humble, thinking of others as better than yourself. Don't think only about your own affairs, but be interested in others, too, and what they are doing. Your attitude should be the same that Christ Jesus had."

The Revelation:

Good morning my child; may this day meet and greet you with the peace, joy and blessings of Heaven. There is nothing more pleasing to me than to see you walking truly and sincerely humble in your daily life. When you are humble, truly humble, you will have a peace that remains while others ridicule and find fault with you. Your humility will keep you focused and fixed on me and not so much on the people and problems around you. The spirit of humility will remind you of your human nothingness and will help you war against all forms of pride and self-righteousness. Whenever you seek to raise yourself up above others people will resent you with tooth and nail but they will have much respect for you when you see yourself as little in your own eyes. A humble saint does not look for admiration. Because of true humility he is willing to be last while others are anxious to be first. A humble saint is not interested in honors, popularity, reputation, or even human applauses. He only seeks my approval because he knows I judge without error or partiality. When you are truly humble you are nor afraid to have others know your shortcomings or correct your mistakes. Never compare yourself with anyone who may seem worse off than you but reflect upon the fact I have found favor with you in a special way. Your humility will remind you daily that you are nothing and that you can do nothing without me. When you see yourself as little in your own eyes, my Father sees you as great in His eyes. Nothing will happen in your life today that I can't handle.

The Response:

Most gracious, wise and all loving God; praise, glory and honor are due to you daily from my lips and heart. I am so thankful to receive another day of living on this planet. As I live out this day, help me to walk honest and humble before you and the world. I never want to consider myself above anyone else. I realize I am nothing without you and all because of you I exist. Grant me a spirit of humility that I might draw closer to you in spirit and in truth. Help me to abandon all pretenses, hypocrisies and false ways and just be humble and open with myself, with you and with those around me. I don't desire to be first, popular or big. I just want to please you by imitating Christ by living a true life. That is my greatest glory. When praises and honor come to me, I shall pass them on to you. Amen.

Day 74

The Reading:

Luke 4:1-2, 13, "Then Jesus, full of the Holy Spirit, left the Jordan River. He was led by the Spirit to go out into the wilderness, where the Devil tempted him for forty days. He ate nothing all that time and was very hungry; When the Devil had finished tempting Jesus, he left him until the next opportunity came."

The Revelation:

Good morning my child and welcome to another ordained and consecrated day. In this life you will experience some serious temptations just for resolving to follow me. You will notice, too, that some of my followers suffer temptations near the end of their life; journey and some will suffer temptation throughout most of their life's journey. Each person will be tempted or allowed to be tempted predicated upon what they can bear. There are those that will be spared any serious temptations and yet they are overcome by small temptations daily. I permit temptations to come to humble you and keep you aware of your weaknesses and not to rely on your own strength. Whenever temptations come to you, I do not want you to despair. Always come to me in prayer and do what you can to avoid the temptation. When you suspect they are coming, always trust in my word and be well assured that I will never allow temptation to tempt you beyond what you can handle. You are never alone when it comes to temptation. All true followers of mine are being tempted daily. Remember even I was tempted by the devil himself all throughout my earthly ministry. I strongly encourage you to fight temptation and resist it with all of your might. When you do, my Father is very pleased; when you increase in spiritual fortitude stay strong and fight on. Nothing will happen in your life today that I can't handle.

The Response:

Dearest God of love and mercy, day after day you prove your agape' love for me. I am blessed beyond measure to inherit another day. It is my joy to receive whatever comes my way today good or bad or indifferent. It is not my desire to complain nor to pity myself. I now understand that trials and temptations come to make me strong. I will not look for trouble or seek out temptations but I will do my best to resist and to face each one in honor of you. Lord, I want to do my best to please you by overcoming my faults and growing in your grace. Amen.

Day 75

The Reading:

Romans 7:15-18 "Don't understand myself at all, for I really want to do what is right, but I don't do it. Instead, I do the very thing I hate. I know perfectly well that what I am doing is wrong, and my bad conscience shows that I agree that the law is good. But I can't help myself, because it is sin inside me that makes me do these evil things. I know I am rotten through and through so far as my old sinful nature is concerned. No matter which way I turn, I can't make myself do right. I want to, but I can't."

The Revelation:

Good morning my child and prepare yourself for the break through blessings that are coming your way today. When man and woman were in the Garden of Eden they were blessed with the gifts from Heaven to make their earthly journey as easy and as peaceful as possible. They had complete control over the appetites and desires of their flesh and soul. In a defiant act of disobedience man and woman disobeyed my command by eating the forbidden fruit. Even though some see this as a small act outwardly but their inferior rebellion against my will was very serious. As a result of their disobedience they forfeited my gifts that brought them soulful peace. Now, all humans on earth have to suffer and endure inner conflict. Even when one wants to do the right thing, his animalistic appetites wars against his better judgment. Because of what happened in the Garden of Eden, you too, have to fight daily for control of your unreasoning and blind desires. Infused knowledge is no longer available at will but now only through daily laboring and experience. Because of the act of disobedience in the Garden of Eden you have conflicted struggles of the mind and will. Nevertheless, to assist you in yielding to what is right and wrong I have provided you with my written word and the privilege of prayer. As long as you are in your humanly state you will always be in conflict with your flesh. Yet you must strive daily to do your best regardless of any sinful desires and temptations. Nothing will happen in your life today that I can't handle.

The Response:

Most Gracious and all loving God—I am grateful for you waking me to another day. I thank you and submit to your holy will as an obedient servant. As I have another opportunity through this day to live for you, I pray that you will help me to conquer the conflicts that go on in my flesh. I know that nothing good lives in me but, I want to correct whatever is evil in my life as much as I have control. It is not my desire to follow the law of sin but to always yield to your word. I want to do what is good and holy. I want to please you. Help me and bless me with the strength to always follow Christ. Amen.

Day 76

The Reading:

Galatians 5:24 "Those who belong to Christ Jesus have nailed the passions and desires of their sinful nature to his cross and crucified them there."

The Revelation:

Good morning my child and may your day be full of peace and joy from Heaven. This is a very special lesson for you today. Before you can truly and sincerely call yourself one of my sold out disciples you must endure and engage a great inner battle daily within your spirit. Your fleshly desires and appetites will not easily surrender themselves to my will. Your flesh desires only one thing, to satisfy itself. There is nothing and I mean nothing on this earth that can compare to my love. In me and through me you will find your greatest advantage and perfect satisfaction. You must always be ready and willing to sacrifice all things that seek to draw and attract you away from me. Out of all your earthly needs, none is greater than the need for you to control your fleshly desires and passions. When you find it hard or even a struggle to obey and submit to the authorities in your life, look beyond them and see me in the situation. I want you to always think clearly and respond humbly; never allow your feelings or flesh or moods to deceive you. With clear thinking, a humble spirit, deep faith in my word and a firm confidence In my help you must always control your life according to my will. This will be your highest achievement. This will be your greatest glory. Of all of your daily deeds none is more important or greater than crucifying your flesh. When you have gained full and complete control over your flesh, you will have gained control over everything else in your life. Blessed and great is the person who has learned to be firm and controlling of their passions and desires. The more perfect you die to yourself the more perfect you can live for me and my Father. Nothing will happen in your life today that I can't handle.

The Response:

Oh Lord, my God and my Saviour. Thanks be unto you for waking me up this morning. Thanks be unto you for your grace and your mercy. Today, I place all that I am and desire at your feet. I choose to follow your will for my life freely and openly. I begin now crucifying my fleshly desires and passions to follow you. It is my desire to submit to your will and follow you in two ways. (1) by embracing to whatever you choose to send me in the way of labors, joys, hardship and (2) by following you deliberately contradicting my passions and desires of the flesh. I pray for spiritual contempt against anything and anyone that stands between my loyalty and love for you. I am completely yours. Amen.

Day 77

The Reading:

2 Chronicles 10:8-9 "But Rehoboam rejected the advice of the elders and instead asked the opinion of the young men who had grown up with him and who were now his advisers. "What is your advice?" he asked them. "How should I answer these people who want me to lighten the burdens imposed by my father?"

The Revelation:

Good morning my child and may the joy of Heaven shower down on you all day. Those who are still infants in the faith will lack experience and maturity in their daily walk towards holiness. Many of them will be easily deceived and duped by the devil unless they listen to and follow the advice of the more mature saints. As for you, you have grown in the faith and are much more mature than an infant. So when temptations upset your peace and you are not sure exactly what path to take go and seek the advice and counsel of a more spiritual saint. Rather than follow your own ideas, prefer to follow the counsel of the older and wiser person in the faith. I have told you before the devil can quote scripture for his own purpose. He can also imitate my inspirations. He is very clever with his deceit. Seek counsel. Never be too proud to ask and follow advice. Study and reflect on the proverbs of the past. They too are full of divine wisdom and direction. After you have sought and received advice humble yourself and follow it. Always try to discern the source of your temptations and then root it out of your life. If not, they will return and your condition will be the same as before if not worse. Never let pride or fear prevent you from seeking advice. Remember my words through James, "If any one lack wisdom, let them ask me who gives it liberally." Nothing will happen in your life today that I can't handle.

The Response:

Gracious God of wisdom and mercy; all praise and honor be unto you. I am thankful for the gift of another day. Truly you are a merciful and gracious God. I pray today for divine wisdom either through your word, through prayer or through the counsel of a wiser saint. Please teach me Lord how to humble myself and seek the advice of those who have the experience and the tried and proven faith. Lord, I want to live not only spiritually but intelligently for you. Throughout this day lead me and guide me to those who are full of wisdom and your Holy Spirit. After I have drunk a mind full of their anointed advice grant me the humility and the courage to follow it. Prepare me right now to be a receptacle of wisdom, knowledge, and truth, for your sake and for your glory. Amen.

The Reflection: [What I heard the Holy Spirit speaking into my spirit during the past seven days and how it changed me or challenged me].

_____

_____

_____

_____

_____

_____

_____

_____

_____

_____

_____

_____

_____

_____

_____

_____

_____

_____

Day 78

The Reading:

Genesis 3:8-9 "Toward evening they heard the Lord God walking about in the garden, so they hid themselves among the trees. The Lord God called to Adam, "Where are you?"

The Revelation:

Good morning my child, I trust that you found sweet sleep and that you are looking forward to another God ordained day. I desire you to seek comfort and ultimate satisfaction from me and me alone. When you do, I will bestow upon you the grace and favor of knowing me and enjoying my fellowship like never before. Your inner peace will never be disturbed again by the daily events you encounter. You will never complain again about what you do not have nor become so attached with what you do have. You will desire me above anything and anyone else. You will discover that I alone am the wellspring of true peace. I encourage you to walk close to me in your daily life. Nothing on this earth can satisfy your hunger for peace like being in true fellowship with me. I alone am the only one who can bring you the perfect happiness you desire and seek daily. This eternal fellowship requires that you stay in a right relationship with me. This means your main desire each day is to give Me all the due attention and time that is possible. Seek me out daily. Don't hide from me. When I call, answer. You only hinder and deprive yourself of my presence and my grace when you hide. I look forward to our time and communion together each day. Without spending some time with me, your day will be imperfect and stressful. Come unto Me daily and walk with me in true fellowship and I will bless you. Nothing will happen in your life today that I can't handle.

The Response:

O' Lord, my God, and my perfect companion; I am indeed thankful and blessed to receive another ordained day in this life. As I begin this day I do so seeking to commune with you in fellowship. I yearn daily to walk in your presence and to remain close to you in holiness. Lord, I never want to hide from you under any circumstance. Teach me to answer you when you call.

Teach me the value of being in your presence on a daily basis. Only you can satisfy me and grant me true peace and happiness. As I journey throughout this day move me to take time out to commune with you. I long to be in your company. Amen.

Day 79

The Reading:

John 14:1 "Don't be troubled. You trust God, now trust in me."

The Revelation:

Good morning my child and welcome to this anointed new day blessed and consecrated just for you. I desire that you believe in me. I am asking that you put all of your trust and hope in my love and my mercy. There are many times I know that when you think I am a distance away from you I am really close to you. There are times when you feel everything is going wrong and you are in it all by yourself. Those are the times my presence is absolutely with you. These are the times, to also prove your faith and loyalty in me as your Lord and Saviour. Just because you experience trials and some times failures does not mean you are a failure. Never judge things by your disappointments or dislikes. I want you to learn how to keep discouragement out of your heart; no matter how hopeless the situation may appear. Always do your best and accept the results as my perfect will. Remember, I am your Lord and I have unconditional love for you. I know your most hidden thoughts. I am interested in only one thing for you—your eternal soul salvation. I have very good reasons for letting you feel disgusted and disinterested in your daily activities. Never complain when you are deprived of something on this earth. You cannot claim anything as your own. All things are mine. When you face trouble, trials and tribulations, it is me allowing them to come upon you. Through them all continue to believe, hope and trust in me. Never let your heart be conjoined with sadness but rejoice in the midst of the circumstance and peace and contentment will be yours. Continue to believe and I will always be there. Nothing will happen in your life today that I can't handle.

The Response:

O' Lord, My God how excellent is thy name in all the earth. Thank you for another days journey and the favor of living out another day to your glory. I freely and willingly accept your will for my life. I submit to you for all things. Whether it is consolation or desolation I desire to serve you as you deserve. I know you are with me in whatever situation I find myself. Teach me to trust in you and to lean on you when I don't understand what I'm going through. You have never forsaken me and all that have confronted me have been for my own good. I know you are all wise and all loving; your will is my will. Amen.

Day 80

The Reading:

Daniel 12:4 "But you, Daniel, keep this prophecy a secret; seal up the book until the time of the end. Many will rush here and there, and knowledge will increase."

The Revelation:

Good morning my child and may the blessings of Heaven be yours for the asking. In this world knowledge is usually the cause of pride and vanity. Many people consider themselves better and more important than others because of their knowledge or intellect. They fail to realize knowledge has no value unless it makes them a better person in their daily life. Knowledge is also the cause of many useless distractions. Most of the knowledge people acquire will make no difference in their life. If those who thirst after knowledge were just as eager to root out evil the planet would be a better place. Some are just interested in being honored than they are being humble. As a result they get lost in their own self-centeredness. They are ruined through vain learning and valueless knowledge because they forget the true service of all wisdom and knowledge. Those who are self-wise are full of pride and are rarely humble. They value themselves or others based upon their knowledge or the lack of it. My child, never forget knowledge is only half the person; action is the other half. The more you learn the more you will discover you are ignorant of many other things in life. True knowledge will humble a person and reveal to him/her the true essence of God's creation. The most educated people are aware that they know very little. When you contend that your education makes you better than your neighbor than you have missed the spirit of true education. True education will show you more and more of God in the world. Know this, unless your knowledge makes you a better person for the glory of God it is a waste of time. Nothing will happen in your life today that I can't handle.

The Response:

God of wisdom, knowledge and truth, thank you for blessing me with the spirit of life to see and live out another day. On this day I yield myself to your foundation of knowledge. Teach me your divine truths and help me to understand that all knowledge should bring me closer to you or otherwise it's all in vain. Grant me wisdom, knowledge and understanding to help make this world a better place for your glory. Let me not waste my time learning any thing that does edify me and glorify your name. Amen.

Day 81

The Reading:

James 1:12 "God blesses the people who patiently endure testing. Afterward they will receive the crown of life that God has promised to those who love him."

The Revelation:

Good morning my child and peace and joy are yours for the asking for the day. Only those who persevere to the end will be saved. By my grace I want you to be determined to follow my will in your life daily. Follow it regardless of your feelings. Your moods and feelings will change from day to day but your will must stand firm in loyalty to me. There are times when you will welcome what I send you and sometimes you will dislike it. There will be times when you will be eager to obey and submit to me and there will be times you will resist it. Your true loyalty and allegiance to me will be proven by your determination to endure the journey towards Heaven. Don't let the Devil deceive you or distract you. Keep your focus fixed on Heaven, which is your goal. Don't let your health, your friends or other people's opinions trouble your spirit and cause you to abandon your course of holiness. While striving to endure your daily trials, your worst enemy will be your own flesh. It will dislike the charge to persevere and follow my direction. But you are to continue to walk in faith, in hope and obedience. Keep yourself engaged in prayer, self-denial and steadfastness. When you do you will find yourself growing stronger in endurance and closer to me in grace. If you don't faint, if you don't quit, if you stand and withstand your trials, you will receive a crown of life. Nothing will happen in your life today that I can't handle.

The Response:

Most Gracious Lord and Saviour, thank you, for watching over me last night and waking me up this morning. I am truly grateful for your mercy. As I press on towards Heaven today, I pray for endurance and patience to stay the course. Please grant me the strength to deal with my daily difficulties and conquer my crosses. My goal is eternity and my desire is to please you. I'm striving daily to earn my crown of life. No matter what the suffering or the hardship; I am willing to endure them. Grant me the grace to keep my eyes on the goal so that I may never become discouraged, distracted, or defeated by my trials in this life. Help me O' Lord to run on to inherit my crown in eternity. Amen.

Day 82

The Reading:

James 1:5 "If you need wisdom—if you want to know what God wants you to do—ask him, and he will gladly tell you. He will not resent your asking."

The Revelation:

Good morning my child and welcome to another ordained day created before the beginning. During this day permit me to teach you some of my heavenly wisdom. The gift of wisdom is more precious than all the silver and gold on earth. One of the main reasons why so many people judge wrongly is because their mindset is limited to the things of this world. They use all kinds of earthly reasoning to defend their judgments and therefore they fall into sin and error. I would not have you to make the same mistakes or be deceived by wrong reasoning. As long as anyone disagrees with my judgment or my will they are wrong. Human reasoning may be better understood than my heavenly judgment but this only proves that my wisdom is far above all created intelligence. You will only insult my wisdom if you prefer human reasoning to my word. Worldly people are foolish and lacking in perfect reasoning. They are not foolish because they value the good things in this life but because they value them too much. Many people fail to see the full truth about themselves; therefore, they get false notions about their greatness. All true greatness is a gift from me, my child. My lesson for you today is to know your true greatness lies in seeking my divine wisdom. For your daily living I desire you to follow my wisdom in all things and for all things. Not everything that looks good is good. This era is filled with conflicting beliefs. The times are confusing. You can avoid the confusion by asking me for wisdom and following my lead. I stand ready to bless you with as much wisdom as you need. Nothing will happen in your life today that I can't handle.

The Response:

My Lord and my God . . . Glory and honor to you. Thanksgiving and praises to you for allowing me to live to see another blessed day. Today I ask and yearn for your wisdom. You are the fountain of all truth and logic. Never again do I want to pursue earthly and worldly reasoning. I now understand that any and all beliefs or philosophies that disagree with you are all wrong. I will try to think more and more about your way daily. I will study to learn your truths better and better. Your wisdom is worth more than all the silver and gold on earth and I prefer it above riches and honor. Grant me your wisdom today as I strive to please you and to follow you in all things. Amen.

Day 83

The Reading:

Psalm 146:3-4, "Don't put your confidence in powerful people; there is no help for you there. When their breathing stops, they return to the earth, and in a moment all their plans come to an end."

The Revelation:

Good morning my child and may your day be filled with the eternal joy of Heaven. Too often many of you depend on human help or worldly remedies to get you through life. Many of you forget that every thing in the world is in my hands and that without me all help is in vain. People of the world put too much trust and hope in their own abilities or the abilities of their friends and family. Many, good health, popular reputation, social admiration and other such things are valued beyond true worth. It is only through me that true value and worth can be attained. It is only through me that the treasure of true peace and eternal joy can come. Whenever you possess me fully and faithfully you possess something and someone that can never be taken away from you. Hold on to Me. Cling to me by faith and never depend too much on the favor of humans to help you. Your greatest and ultimate hope should always be in me. My love for you will assist you, and sustain you and save you where human associates fail and are powerless. The powers and people you depend on outside of me will be short lived. I alone can give the unending love and the never ceasing joy that will make your life complete. When you live only for what this life can offer, you will soon meet with great disappointment. Always trust and hope in me and you will live. Nothing will happen in your life today that I can't handle.

The Response:

Most excellent and everlasting God—I give you praise, honor and thanksgiving for your many blessings. Most specifically, I thank you for allowing me to see and live another day. It is in you I put all of my trust, hopes and desires. Please never let me treasure or trust anything or anyone that can take me away from you. No friend, no relative, no created thing can take your place in my life. Stay near me throughout this day and teach me how to live my life depending upon you alone. Teach me how to always seek you first and trust in you in everything. My hope is built on nothing less—than you Lord. Amen.

Day 84

The Reading:

Ecclesiastes 1:12-14 "I, the Teacher, was king of Israel, and I lived in Jerusalem. I devoted myself to search for understanding and to explore by wisdom everything being done in the world. I soon discovered that God has dealt a tragic existence to the human race. Everything under the sun is meaningless, like chasing the wind."

The Revelation:

Good morning my child. This is the day that my Father has created, be happy and rejoice during its hours. Today I want you to learn from the folly and mistakes of those who are yet worldly. Notice how hard they take their losses. After a loss, they labor and struggle without end to regain their losses but yet they so easily forget about their spiritual losses. Many of them are so interested in gaining that which has no value and forsake those things, which are important. My child, unless you fight daily to control your thoughts and desires, you too, will be distracted and enslaved by the temporal things in this world. How foolish are those who do not realize their struggles are like chasing after the wind. They would rather chase after that which is forever fleeting and passing then to desire heaven. Most of them would rather stay on earth, going in circles then to cling to the cross of Christ and someday be with Him in eternity. Do not become foolish and blind like these people. In a short while they will come to the end of this earthly life and be no more. But you, if you would learn from their folly and foolishness and keep the faith—the eternal things will be yours forever and you would have gained the greatest earthly treasure of all, divine wisdom. Only a fool would pass up wisdom. Nothing will happen in your life today that I can't handle.

The Response:

O' Lord, my God, the Father of all wisdom and intelligence; I greet you this morning with thanksgiving in my heart. Again, you have blessed me to see another day and I am eternally grateful. I pray throughout this day that I am not found guilty of chasing after those things that have no eternal value. Let me face life's greatest fact and conclusion—the ultimate destiny for each of us is Heaven or Hell. The things I pursue in this life will show the choice I'm making for the next life. Grant me the strength to desire only the holy things that matter and the wisdom to separate myself from anything else that has no eternal value. Pour out your wisdom on me this day and fill me with your eternal insights. Amen.

The Reflection: [What I heard the Holy Spirit speaking into my spirit during the past seven days and how it changed me or challenged me].

_____

_____

_____

_____

_____

_____

_____

_____

_____

_____

_____

_____

_____

_____

By faith, I want to find favor with you like the prophets and patriarchs of old. Help me to continue to honor you with faith and action. I know a little faith will get my soul into Heaven, but a lot of faith will get Heaven into my soul. Amen.

Day 85

The Reading:

Hebrews 11:5-6 "It was by faith that Enoch was taken up to heaven without dying—" suddenly he disappeared because God took him. "But before he was taken up, he was approved as pleasing to God. So, you see, it is impossible to please God without faith. Anyone who wants to come to him must believe that there is a God and that he rewards those who sincerely seek him."

The Revelation:

Good morning my child, peace and joy are yours today just for the asking. As a disciple and follower of mine, please don't ever respond to the unpleasant things, which come your way with a rebellious spirit. A true person of faith believes my word and submits to my teachings no matter what the confrontation is. This person will follow my lead by faith in all things and at all times. Your faith will help you, my child, to keep your peace and stay calm and cool even when others are trying to unsettle you. When hardships and heartaches come your way. Even if they seem unjust and foolish—keep your faith and walk close to me. Do not depend on your own judgment but learn to call on me and counsel with my Holy Spirit through prayer and my word during your difficult days. I desire you to be a person of faith and vision in your daily life. Walk with me for I am ever near, ever present and ever helping you in all situations. With this kind of faith your soul will not be disturbed or consumed by fear. As a person of faith, the external forces of the world will not easily fool you. By faith, you will be able to discern that which is evil. By faith, you will receive even that which may conflict you as a perfecting of your faith from God. According to your faith you will receive and achieve what you believe. Nothing will happen in your life today that I can't handle.

The Response:

My God and my Savior; all praises and honor be unto you for your kindness and mercy in allowing me to witness another day and to serve you throughout this day. As I engage this new day I pray for a deeper faith in knowing you and serving you. I desire to yield to your teachings and leading in my life.

Day 86

The Reading:

1 Peter 1:6-7 "So be truly glad! There is wonderful joy ahead, even though it is necessary for you to endure many trials for a while. These trials are only to test your faith, to show that it is strong and pure. It is being tested as fire tests and purifies gold—and your faith is far more precious to God than mere gold. So if your faith remains strong after being tried by fiery trials, it will bring you much praise and glory and honor on the day when Jesus Christ is revealed to the whole world."

The Revelation:

Good morning my child; may you receive the grace and favor extended to you on this day. People easily become discouraged by the trials of this life when they don't know my plans. Yes, this life on earth is short and hardly ever free from grief and troubles. You will often be confronted by sins, evil desires, fears, vanities and temptations and trials. You will seldom be without attractions and sorrows in this life. As soon as one trial or one trouble leaves, another one shows up. Yet, in spite of all of these trials and troubles there are those who still live only for this life and seek their delight in it. But I want you to keep a smile on your face and keep the faith through all of your trials and darkness. Never fix your eyes on your present trials but stay focused on the main purpose of your life. Look beyond the horizon of your hardship and see the soon breaking of the dawn. Don't allow your trials to cloud the sunshine of your joy or discourage you from the faith. If you don't submit to your trials you will possess the true liberty of Heaven without any pain, without any heartache and without any sorrow. Yes, you will find this life is short and full of dissatisfaction but Heaven awaits you with a reward that you can't even begin to imagine. Nothing will happen in your life today that I can't handle.

The Response:

O' Lord, my healer and my friend, thanks be unto you for watching over me last night and for waking me again to another anointed and beautiful day. Lord, I know my trials come only to make me strong and to prepare me for eternity. I know every trial, every trouble, and every sorrow is permitted in my life by your infinite wisdom. Only you now what I need to make me strong in the faith and to keep me humble. I ask that you will make me unselfish enough to follow your commands and submissive enough to yield to your plans whether my life be filled with misery or prosperity. I love you Lord and through it all—when this earthly life is over I want to see and live with Jesus forever. It is my desire to please you by passing the test of faith. Amen.

Day 87

The Reading:

Matthew 6:13, "And don't let us yield to temptation, but deliver us from the evil one."

The Revelation:

Good morning my child; I pray that you found sweet sleep as well as welcomed the dawning of this new day. I want you to know that there is absolutely no one who is so perfect and so holy that they do not experience temptations. No one is free from temptation. Many saints, old and new have passed and are passing through the waters of trouble and temptations daily. They use these experiences to exercise their faith and to remain focus on me. Those who did not and do not stand up and fight temptations were defeated by them. I do not want you to become disturbed because things may not be going the way you would have them to go. Look upon each trial and temptation as a part of your journey through life. Temptations will come and go at any hour or day during your life. No time or place is absolutely free from temptations and every person will experience them. However, when your temptations come, I am near you to bless you with the strength to stand and withstand against them. It will be during these times of temptations that you can prove your faith in me and your loyalty for me. During these times of temptations you can practice depending on me, and not your self for strength. Always remember this, temptation is the lot of every person. No one is free from them. My desire is for you to resist and not yield to any of them and to call on me for help when you are confronted by temptation. Be strong and yield not. Nothing will happen in your life today that I can't handle.

The Response:

Dearest Heavenly Father and sustainer of life; I give you absolute praise and thanksgiving for blessing me with another day on this planet. As I live out this day grant me your strength and grace not to yield to any temptations. I know there is no place or time secure from temptation. I know that even Jesus was tempted. Help me to be strong like my Lord was. Help me to stay focused on Heaven and loyal to the faith. When temptations do come, help me to recognize what they are truly designed to do. Whether they come to distract me or destroy me, I love you and I desire to please you daily. I want to become better acquainted with your word and your ways. Nothing is higher than this. Help me to be loyal to you and not yield to sin. Amen.

Day 88

The Reading:

John 16:20-22 "Truly, you will weep and mourn over what is going to happen to me, but the world will rejoice. You will grieve, but your grief will suddenly turn to wonderful joy when you see me again. It will be like a woman experiencing the pains of labor. When her child is born, her anguish gives place to joy because she has brought a new person into the world. You have sorrow now, but I will see you again; then you will rejoice, and no one can rob you of that joy."

The Revelation:

Good morning my child and may the blessings of Heaven shower upon you all day. Hear my words well today; this old world is not your home. You were made for an unending life of perfect happiness with me and my Father in Heaven. This world is not a place of peace but of toil and labor. Never think you have found true peace because things seem to run smoothly for a while. True peace is given to those who know how to face adversity and endure hardships. Let your life be my model on earth. Remember from the cradle to the cross, I patiently endured and encountered all kinds of adversities grief and want were never strangers to me. Ingratitude was my reward for my grace and mercy. You, too, my child will find and face much adversity. Joy will come to you in the midst of it all if you exercise your faith, your humility and your love for me. All of the adversities on earth are nothing compared to the reward that awaits you in Heaven. Never complain but press on with joy in the time of your adversity. Remember, what Paul wrote; "The suffering of this present time are not worthy to be compared with the glory to come [Romans 8:18]." Your adversity and grief are but for a little while. Keep the faith and be obedient unto death and joy will be eternally yours. Nothing will happen in your life today that I can't handle.

The Response:

My Lord, my God and my inspiration, thank you for another day's journey. Thank you for keeping me and watching over me during the night. I've come to learn that true and lasting joy will only come when I inherit Heaven. In this life I must suffer and have sorrow. I want to live like Jesus and endure hardship like He did. I now know the worst thing in this life is not suffering or hardship or grief but sin. Help me today to see the eternal good that lies in suffering and trials. Let my suffering remind me of what Jesus went through for my sins. I pray today that I never look upon suffering and adversity again as something to be hated or disliked but as a school of faith perfecting. Amen.

Day 89

The Reading:

Matthew 5:46-48 "If you love only those who love you, what good is that? Even corrupt tax collectors do that much. If you are kind only to your friends, how are you different from anyone else? Even pagans do that. But you are to be perfect, even as your Father in heaven is perfect."

The Revelation:

Good morning my child and welcome to another blessed and anointed day ordained before the beginning of time. I desire for you to strive daily to live and love with a spirit of perfection. If you only knew what was in store for you in Heaven you would gladly endure and welcome any trial or suffering that come your way. However, I don't want you to just go through life because of your eternal reward. No, I want you to live holy and perfect with the purest motives because of your love and loyalty for me. During your daily journey always look for opportunities to contradict and challenge your own selfishness. In during so, you will prove your spiritual growth and progress. Always be aware of self-deception and self-seeking within your spirit. Root out all of these motives by constantly contradicting them with holiness and perfection. In doing this, never neglect to be obedient to those who rule over you with authority. Your obedience will be a sure sign of spiritual perfection. Even still, avoid false virtue. Never do anything or say anything that will negate your holiness or striving for perfection. Be ready to have your virtue tested by daily experiences you encounter in life. Do not fear failure or misunderstandings or sufferings. The only thing to fear is only have lived this day without growing spiritually in any way. You will never reach me without yielding yourself completely and unreservingly to my will. Nothing will happen in your life today that I can't handle.

The Response:

Most Gracious and Holy Lord, I am thankful for the blessing of this new day. It is my desire to walk and talk holy as a child of yours. I offer you my unreserved obedience and allegiance to live as your word dictates. Fix my mind so completely on your holiness and perfection that I may hunger for one thing and that is to contradict myself for you. All I want and deeply desire is to give you all that I am and all that I have. I want to imitate Jesus in my holiness and quest for perfection. Amen.

Day 90

The Reading:

Matthew 25:31-34 "But when the Son of Man comes in his glory, and all the angels with him, then he will sit upon his glorious throne. All the nations will be gathered in his presence, and he will separate them as a shepherd separates the sheep from the goats. He will place the sheep at his right hand and the goats at his left. Then the King will say to those on the right, 'Come, you who are blessed by my Father, inherit the Kingdom prepared for you from the foundation of the world.'"

The Revelation:

Good morning my child and welcome to another wonderful day ordained and anointed before the beginning. My child I crafted and created you for the perfect holiness and happiness of Heaven. When you strive to be Holy to inherit Heaven you please my father and me. Yes, there are many who desire Heaven for different reasons. Regardless of the reason if anyone shows any degree of loving me and wanting to please me they are on the road to inheriting Heaven. What I require of you and all of my followers is not a feeling or an emotion. I require obedience and love for m truths. The first truth is that I am the Son of God; the way, the truth and the life. All are expected to live their lives based on this first truth. Those who love me and my truth and desire to inherit Heaven can be divided into three groups. (1) Those who love me only to avoid hell. (2) Those who love me enough by surrendering themselves occasionally to my will and (3) Those who offer and submit themselves to me completely. They imitate me in their daily lives and I am their only example. This last group is pure in heart and only desire to please me in everything. Strive to be like them in your daily walk, and Heaven will be yours at the end of this earth's journey. Nothing will happen in your life today that I can't handle.

The Response:

O' Lord my God and my life, thank you for the blessing and the gift of another day. Each day is a cherish treasure. I pray as I live this day that my ways are pleasing to you. I desire to glorify your name in all I say and do. Even as I yearn for Heaven—I want to live and serve you while still on this planet. My desire is not to just miss hell but to honor you and favor your will. As I walk toward eternal life let each step I take represent unconditional obedience and submission. I want to hear you say well done—good and faithful servant. Yes, I desire Heaven but I desire to love you and follow you while in this world much more. Amen.

Day 91

The Reading:

Colossians 3:1-4 "Since you have been raised to new life with Christ, set your sights on the realities of heaven, where Christ sits at God's right hand in the place of honor and power. Let heaven fill your thoughts. Do not think only about things down here on earth. For you died when Christ died, and your real life is hidden with Christ in God. And when Christ, who is your real life, is revealed to the whole world, you will share in all his glory."

The Revelation:

Good morning my child and may the blessings of Heaven fulfill your daily desires. As you seek to share in fellowship with me through prayer, reading the word and fasting, you will become like me daily. Your actions will be transformed. Your old self will slowly and gradually take on a god-self and my outlook on life will replace yours. As you continue to seek that which is holy and eternal you will begin, too, to share in my desires, my intentions and my divine dignity. In essence, your earthly life will be an extension of me. You will have the same privilege to petition my Father as I had. He will grant you every petition for my sake. Now, that your life is hidden in mine and you have the same power and privileges of me—you will be a blessing to others and yourself. For this reason Satan will oppose you and attack you. If he can't gain your soul, he will attempt to stop you from blessing others. However, your fellowship with me will weaken his temptations. As you continue to seek those things that represent Heaven—you will become an effective soldier of mine. Thus, you must never grow weary of seeking divine help and guidance. As you serve me on earth you will share in my glory in Heaven. Nothing will happen in your life today that I can't handle.

The Response:

Most gracious and all wise God—I am grateful for another day under Heaven. You have been very merciful to me. I thank you for that. As I live this day, I am seeking those things, which are from above. I am setting my mind on those things that are holy and eternal. I pray that my thoughts, my desires and all of my intentions are heavenly centered. Let my life be a life that seeks to serve others like Christ did. As His life was a channel and source of salvation use me in the same way. The more I hide myself in Christ, the more I become like Christ. My goal today is to become more and more like Christ. My goal today is to seek those things which are from above and to live them out daily. Make me as you would have me to be. Amen.

The Reflection: [What I heard the Holy Spirit speaking into my spirit during the past seven days and how it changed me or challenged me].

_____

_____

_____

_____

_____

_____

_____

_____

_____

_____

_____

_____

_____

_____

Day 92

The Reading:

Galatians 6:1-3, "Dear brothers and sisters, if another Christian is overcome by some sin, you who are godly should gently and humbly help that person back onto the right path. And be careful not to fall into the same temptation yourself. Share each other's troubles and problems, and in this way obey the law of Christ. If you think you are too important to help someone in need, you are only fooling yourself. You are really a nobody."

The Revelation:

Good morning my child and may the favor of Heaven smile upon you all day. It is my will and desire to fill your heart to overflowing with a full and perfect love. This is so, as you serve others you will always do it for my sake. Please be good and do good to all—but refuse to sin for anyone. There should never be any excuse for doing what is wrong and disappointing me. However, there may be times when you may have to put your religious duties on hold for a while in order to help some one. When this happens you are still pleasing me. When someone is not interested in the needs of a neighbor they are not interested in me. For my sake always reach out to help others as much as you can. In your willingness to help someone else please be careful in growing impatience when things don't turn out the way you wish. If the person you are assisting insists on continuing in their ways of error—pray for them and leave them to me. If all people were perfect you would have little to suffer for my sake. Each person has their faults and their burdens. You ought to bear one another's burdens, you ought to help one another, you ought to console one another, and you ought to warn one another. Treat each other as you would want me to treat you. In doing so you are proving your love for Me. Nothing will happen in your Life today that I can't handle.

The Response:

O' Lord, my Savior, thank you for last night sleep and slumber, and for this mornings uprising. It is indeed a blessing to see another morning. I love you Lord, and to prove my love, I seek to help others who are burdened and troubled. Grant me your grace today—that I may perfectly reflect your patience and desire to reach out to others. Never let me think more of myself than what I truly am. Never let me forsake to aid or assist a falling neighbor. I pray that I may be merciful to them as you are always merciful to me. Let my love for you be proven by my actions toward others. Amen.

Day 93

The Reading:

John 5:24 "I assure you, those who listen to my message and believe in God who sent me have eternal life. They will never be condemned for their sins, but they have already passed from death into life."

The Revelation:

Good morning my child, and welcome to another day prepared just for you and your spiritual development. When you believe my words you are endowed with the truth. I first spoke to this world through man's conscience, then I spoke to the world through my prophets, then I spoke to the world through my earthly ministry and now I speak to the world through my institution called the church. The church, my child, is my voice, my authority and my covenant community. The church is the only voice that I ordained and consecrated to carry own my work and my words. When you believe in my church and its mission, you believe in me. My church is in place in the earth to teach my truths. Never become discouraged or dismayed when you don't understand all that the church is called to do. Just remain faithful and obedient. I am guiding the church by my Spirit. Besides, human reason is too weak and too finite to grasp all that I am divinely capable of doing. That is why I have empowered and enlightened my church with the truth to teach you and to inform you of those things that are eternal when it comes to hearing, receiving and believing my word. I do not demand great intelligence. I only ask that you have faith in my word, my church and my prophets. Just be loyal to our fellowship and my will. I will never deny my grace to any person who is willing to pray, labor and believe in my word by faith. Nothing will happen in your life today that I can't handle.

The Response:

Greetings, most gracious Lord and God of all truth, thank you for favoring me to see another day. I am truly blessed and forgiven by you. By faith dear Lord, I accept and believe your holy word. By faith, I am obedient to your church and its spiritual leaders. I will never doubt your word or your will as revealed through the church, which represents and speaks for you. I believe today more than ever in your word and I submit to your word as my guiding compass towards eternal truth. I pray that I will never tire of believing in your word or following the faith to the end. I desire to prove my faith and what I believe by my continual obedience to serve you better and grow perfectly in my daily life. May I never become foolish to believe in anything or anyone outside of your word. Your word is the truth and I believe it. Amen!!!

Day 94

The Reading:

John 15:12-15 "I command you to love each other in the same way that I love you. And here is how to measure it—the greatest love is shown when people lay down their lives for their friends. You are my friends if you obey me. I no longer call you servants, because a master doesn't confide in his servants. Now you are my friends, since I have told you everything the Father told me."

The Revelation:

Good morning my child, I pray that you are receiving and rejoicing in spirit for this new day. Think about how many friends you really have that will stand by you and with you when you really need them. How many friends do you have will make sacrifices of their busy schedules to support you? No matter how dear people say they are with you and for you, you still live your daily life basically alone. In the middle of the night, in moments of tiredness; when others are busy looking out for themselves, this is when you experience the reality of being alone and unnoticed by others. Never over estimate your friendship with others. Sooner or later you will have to leave them or they will leave you. If you depend too much on human relationships you will have to endure a painful separation some day. Even human friendship needs my anointing. Always encourage your friends to draw near to me daily by being a good example of holiness. With my blessing and the staying power of my Holy Spirit your earthly friendships can be an eternal thing. All friendships must be predicated on virtue, loyalty and integrity to me. Anyone who suggests sin to you is not your friend. Nothing will happen in your life today that I can't handle.

The Response:

Most gracious, and all loving God, I rise this morning to say thank you for your loving kindness and forgiveness. You have blessed me to see another day and I am grateful. As I go about this day I pray that I will first and foremost honor Jesus as my best and holy friend. There is no one who can have as noble of a friend like Jesus. When it comes to my earthly friends help me not to depend on them as much as I should depend on Jesus, my true friend. I desire to be an example to my earthly friends and always represent holiness before them. But, Jesus is my perfect friend and my eternal friend and all others must take second place. Amen

Day 95

The Reading:

2 Thessalonians 3:16, "May the Lord of peace himself always give you his peace no matter what happens. The Lord be with you all."

The Revelation:

Good morning my child and may the perfect peace of Heaven be your companion throughout this day. Always know when you have been granted the grace to think in my ways—you will never again fall into sadness. Most people become sad because they are deprived of something they really want. If you desire me above any created thing, only sin and selfishness will make you sad. If you truly follow me, you will live in peace. Do not become troubled because something or someone is against you. It will not be the first time or the last time. As a matter of fact, more is said behind your back than what you will ever hear. Never lose any sleep over the judgment of people. Do your best to please me and you will know peace. Never let worry or anxiety consume you. I do not expect you to do the impossible. *Stop demanding of yourself more than I demand of you.* It is pride that makes you desire immediate perfection. The humble seeks perfection within his/her own strength and ability. That person does his/her best to simply renew themselves when they fail. You will have perfect peace when you stop deceiving yourself that you are perfect and demanding more than you can possibly do. Let me guide you through the trials of your daily life and if you would embrace my will along the way, peace will be yours. Nothing will happen in your life today that I can't handle.

The Response:

O Lord, my God how excellent is your name, your love and your grace in all the earth. Blessings and honor are given to you for my gift of another day. Grant me the perfect peace of Heaven as I live out this day. Walk near me ever so close as I journey throughout today. Teach me how to embrace your will and submit to your guidance. I desire to do what I can within my strength to please you and strive toward perfection. If I fail today in anything teach me to renew myself and seek your guidance to begin again. While trying to reach Heaven, I do not want to sin in any way. Grant me the peace and patience to do my best to please you. Grant me the grace to love holiness and hate sin. I desire to live in peace until Heaven is my home. Amen.

Day 96

The Reading:

1 Peter 3:17, "Remember, it is better to suffer for doing good, if that is what God wants, than to suffer for doing wrong!"

The Revelation:

Good morning my child and may you receive this anointed and new day with joy and rejoicing. I want you to understand on this day as long as you are afraid to suffer you will not possess perfect peace. Your fears to suffer will make it difficult for you to follow my will and submit to my ways. As a result you will slip into sin and do what is spiritually unhealthy for you. If you desire the happiness of Heaven while on earth, you must be loyal to me as your Lord. Be loyal, whether what comes is favorable or unfavorable to your desires. I want you to live your life daily with boldness and bravery even when it involves hardship, heartaches and suffering. When sufferings come do not blame the place where you are nor blame the people around you for the suffering of your soul. If you leave to go else where, you will still be the same, with the same faults, the same sins and the same defects. You might become a change person by leaving but you will not become a better person. As soon as another issue comes up you will have to fight the same battle from which you thought you were running from. To become better means to overcome your faults. If you are afraid to suffer you will never reach spiritual maturity. As you begin today to suffer for my sake, my grace will support and strengthen you. Nothing will happen in your life today that I can't handle.

The Response:

Dear Lord and Savior, I greet you with gratitude and thanksgiving in my heart for another day of life on this earth. I thank you, too, for the example of successful suffering through Jesus Christ. I pray that I will emulate Christ's example through my life. I do not want to avoid those suffering situations, which are vital to my growth and development spiritually. I pray that I will by your grace face them as Christ did. I don't want to let you down but please you and find favor with you. Teach me the virtue of suffering for the sake of Christ. Teach me to represent your goodness and grace in the midst of every trial. Amen.

Day 97

The Reading:

Proverbs 12:1, "To learn, you must love discipline; it is stupid to hate correction."

The Revelation:

Good morning my child and welcome to the grace of God. May His love be obvious to you all throughout this day. On your quest for knowledge know that it is a good thing but unless your knowledge helps you to become a better and holy person it is not good. A simple person who follows and obeys my Word is far better than a professor with many academic degrees, who does not care about my statues. Remember, your daily life is a journey onward and upward towards eternity. The first and most important knowledge is that which aid you in gaining Heaven. The more you learn of my word, my doctrine and me the better you become. All other knowledge is just a supplement to helping you live a holier and useful life. There are those who acquire knowledge for the sole purpose of being esteemed as some great intellectual. If they would spend more time rooting out their faults, correcting their shortcomings and living holy, they would be much better off than they are with all of their knowledge. My child, it is better to be great than merely to be considered great. You will indeed be great if you would grow in the knowledge of my word and learn how to apply them in your daily life. Just talking about a holy life may impress others, but remember, I know people for what and who they really are. Never forget, knowledge is only valuable if it makes you holier and better prepared to receive my grace. Nothing will happen in your life today that I can't handle.

The Response:

All wise and all knowing Father and Creator of all, I greet you with thanksgiving and gratitude in my heart for the blessing of this wonderful morning. Thank you for allowing me to see it and experience it. As I experience this day teach me and show me how to live what I learn through your word. It is better to live your word than to preach them eloquently or to teach them profoundly. I realize the person who can quote your scriptures is not as great as the person who lives them out daily. Expose me to the knowledge that makes me self-centered and despise others. That knowledge is bad for me. I only desire the knowledge that makes me virtuous and holy. Let no other knowledge ever obscure my thirst for the true knowledge of you. Amen.

Day 98

The Reading:

James 5:10-11, "For examples of patience in suffering, dear brothers and sisters, look at the prophets who spoke in the name of the Lord. We give great honor to those who endure under suffering. Job is an example of a man who endured patiently. From his experience we see how the Lord's plan finally ended in good, for he is full of tenderness and mercy."

The Revelation:

Good morning my child and welcome to another anointed day created before the foundation of the world. It is wonderful to know how well you plan and arrange your daily duties but you will still need opportunities to develop and exercise patience. No one can eliminate the unexpected or prepare for the unforeseen and unavoidable. The best remedy or shall we say weapon is patience. Every person on the planet has his share of trials and troubles. The trouble may come in bodily pain, disappointment, spiritual suffering, or just feeling abandoned or all alone. Then there will be times when you become a bother and a burden to yourself. Everybody would like to be free of these trials but it cannot be. Trials and troubles are a part of this life. Wherever you turn, wherever you go, you will always find my cross in one form or another. Your patience will help you keep your soul at peace so that you may continue to walk toward Heaven in times of trials. In times of trouble and trials, your key to peace and joy is patience. Even still, I am with you. Nothing will happen in your life today that I can't handle.

The Response:

O' Lord, my God and my Redeemer, I greet you with praise and thanksgiving in my heart this morning. Thank you for keeping me through the night. Thank you for waking me up this morning. I worship you and honor you as my Lord. As I live out this day help me to embrace my suffering and trials as you did. You mantled a throne of shame and agony for my sins without complaint. I desire to share your cross in my daily life. Teach me how to be patient and accept those things which confront my peace and my joy. Make me more like you. There is no greater glory than to live a life like yours. May I forever honor you through the life I live and give for your sake. Amen.

The Reflection: [What I heard the Holy Spirit speaking into my spirit during the past seven days and how it changed me or challenged me].

_____

_____

_____

_____

_____

_____

_____

_____

_____

_____

_____

_____

_____

_____

_____

_____

_____

_____

_____

Day 99

The Reading:

James 4:1-3 "What is causing the quarrels and fights among you? Isn't it the whole army of evil desires at war within you? You want what you don't have, so you scheme and kill to get it. You are jealous for what others have, and you can't possess it, so you fight and quarrel to take it away from them. And yet the reason you don't have what you want is that you don't ask God for it. And even when you do ask, you don't get it because your whole motive is wrong—you want only what will give you pleasure."

The Revelation:

Good morning my child and may the peace of Heaven be your companion today. The moment you desire and long for anything too much, you forfeit and forsake my peace for you. Those who are proud and covetous are never at peace. If it is the person who is poor in spirit and humble that enjoy a heavenly peace within the soul. To set your life in order, you must first begin within yourself. Only allow yourself to want what I want you to have. Do not desire what is not for you. Do not desire those things which will only tie your heart to this world. When you surrender yourself and your desires to my will—you will gain a victory over all worldly desires and things. Always examine your motives and your desires for wanting anything. Even when what you desire seem holy and good, they too can demand too much of your attention. It is my desire for you to daily love my wisdom and chase my will, thus you will never be downcast or depressed if your plans or others fail you. I am pleased with you when you do your best; let that be your daily desire, to please me. All other desires and intentions can make you fall into sin and lose focus of heaven. Nothing will happen in your life today that I can't handle.

The Response:

Most Gracious Lord God and Merciful Redeemer, I am truly blessed to see another day. I am too grateful for you sustaining my life through the night. As I begin this day given to me, I desire to seek those things that only please you. I know and now realize as long as I desire what you want I will act safely and avoid coveting and sinning. Grant me the patience to take my time and not to rush what must be done slowly and over time. I do not wish to obtain that which is not for me nor that which does not bring you glory. In all things that I desire, I pray that it is with the right motive and that they do not demand or distract me from your will. Bless me with the power to do my best. The rest depends on others and your grace. Let me never think that I am more than what I truly am or desire that which is not for me. Amen.

Day 100

The Reading:

Isaiah 29:13, "And so the Lord says, "These people say they are mine. They honor me with their lips, but their hearts are far away. And their worship of me amounts to nothing more than human laws learned by rote.""

The Revelation:

Good morning my child and may your day be filled with Heaven's joy. As you continue to grow closer to me, and you will soon discover that there are those among the fellowship that have me on their lips but not in their hearts. Some express their devotion to me through prayers, singing and others signs. Yes, some of their rituals are good but they do not prove true devotion to me. They are simply means to help people practice divine devotion. Your daily discipline is useless if they do not influence your holy behavior and thoughts. Your devotion to me is should not be based on feelings or emotions. True devotion to me is an intentional act of respect, reverence and loyalty. Your genuine devotion must be attached to my will. You must be committed to pleasing me in all that you do. As you prove your sincere loyalty, I will grant you more and more of my grace. As a result, you will advance daily in perfection and acting more like me. As a loyal follower of mine you will learn to live with less and less of the world's possessions. I desire you to spend much time in prayer and much works. Thus, you will find your time spent with me is only short. A longing to spend more and more time with me will burn and yearn within your heart. Still all of your practices are only external and will never within themselves make you holy. The measuring rod of your loyalty and devotion to me can only be found in keeping my commandments. Nothing will happen in your life today that I can't handle.

The Response:

Dear Lord, my God, thank you for the grace of life and sustaining that life. I am blessed to be the recipient of another day. I want my day to be filled with true devotion and loyalty towards you. I pray that my allegiance will prove to be whole and true in my relationship with you. I love you Lord and will endeavor to keep your commandments daily to prove it. Amen.

Day 101

The Reading:

Matthew 6:24 "No one can serve two masters. For you will hate one and love the other, or be devoted to one and despise the other. You cannot serve both God and money."

The Revelation:

Good morning my child and welcome to another God ordained day. As you live out this day, I pray that you will strive very strongly to love me and honor me in all of your activities. Never let anyone or anything come between your loyalty for me. If I am considered your main interest and your highest goal then you must forsake all other created things which may attract you from me. Especially anything or anyone that may seduce you into sin. When you separate yourself from such things or such people, your thoughts and desires will no longer be influenced by foolish interests, selfish ambitions or evil desires. Do not seek the standards of worldly people. Depend solely on me and our relationship for soul satisfaction. You cannot serve me faithfully with a divided loyalty. Either I will be your Lord of all or I'm not your Lord at all. This includes your mind, your resources, your ambitions and your wealth. I will be insulted if you make me compete with any of these worldly things for your attention, allegiance and love. No one is worthy of me until he/she has learned to live and love me as his or her highest goal. I must always be the first and highest desire of your soul. Any other way will not only prove that you are double minded but you are also trying to serve two masters. Make me the desire of your heart and highest objective and I will sustain you with my grace. Nothing will happen in your life today that I can't handle.

The Response:

Most Gracious Lord and liberator of life, I am thankful and grateful for your kindness and mercy. Again, you have spared my life to see another day. I desire to honor you and worship you as the Lord of my life. I never want anything or anybody to replace you as first place in my life. There is nothing in this life that can compare with your love, your favor and your mercy. During this day, teach me to serve you, honor you and esteem you as you deserve as my Lord. I want to be worthy of your grace. Let nothing attract or distract my loyalty from you as my king and conqueror. Amen.

Day 102

The Reading:

Isaiah 55:6-7 "Seek the Lord while you can find him. Call on him now while he is near. Let the people turn from their wicked deeds. Let them banish from their minds the very thought of doing wrong! Let them turn to the Lord that he may have mercy on them. Yes, turn to our God, for he will abundantly pardon."

The Revelation:

Good morning my child and may Heaven's favor bless you abundantly today. Always know that when I am with you nothing will be too difficult. When you seek me, you will not need the consolations of anyone else. When I am silent, no human words will ever be able to console or comfort you. I am truly your all and all you need; when you earnestly seek me you will realize this even more. My child you have achieved a great thing when you learn how to converse with me. I favor those who are humble and simple. I enjoy speaking with those who do not have any false intentions or ideas of self-importance. When you seek me and draw near to me you will learn that my message is very easily understood and will not complicate your life. When you call upon me in your time of need before you seek human remedies, I am very pleased. This shows that you are putting your confidence in my power and me. When I am your focus and you concentrate on me nothing will distract you or allure you from me. Apart from me, you will never accomplish anything of substance or value. Know that I am readily available to conference with you in all matters. As you refuse to rely on others and yourself and depend more on my love, and me the closer you will draw to me. Seek me daily for your soul satisfaction and your desires will be fulfilled. Nothing will happen in your life today that I can't handle.

The Response:

O' Lord, my God and my redeemer, you keep on doing great things for me. You woke me up and started me on my way on this, another day. I want you to know that you are the center of my life and that my heart's desire is solely of you. I pray that I will never separate myself from you by depending and seeking human remedies and solutions. It is my daily desire to seek you first and foremost and follow your lead as you guide me. Thank you for allowing me to call on you and seek you as my Savior and friend. May I forever forsake wickedness and embrace your truth. Lord, you are my greatest joy. Amen.

Day 103

The Reading:

Philippians 3:10-11 "As a result, I can really know Christ and experience the mighty power that raised him from the dead. I can learn what it means to suffer with him, sharing in his death, so that, somehow, I can experience the resurrection from the dead."

The Resurrection:

Good morning my child; may the desires of your heart be yours throughout the day. If you wish to know and understand the secret of suffering for my sake and still have peace and joy; you must meditate often on my suffering and trials. When you bury yourself in my life you will draw strength for your trials. When you place your heart and soul within mine you will be filled with love that can endure all things. When you come to me and enter into my heart you will find the strength and the comfort for your daily struggles and trials. When other people slight you or neglect you, it will not bother you. When other people speak ill and evil of you, you will remain calm and peaceful in the midst of it all. Enduring all this will give you a deeper understanding and appreciation of all I went through at the hands of evil, during my earthly life. In my greatest hour of need, I was abandoned and deserted by my friends. But for the love of you and the world, I allowed myself to be despised and abused to suffer untold agony. Now, will you complain when you go through similar circumstances? I had enemies who said many evil things against me and about me. Now, will you grieve when others ridicule you and speak maliciously against you? If you truly desire to know me and reign with me, you must suffer with me and like me. Nothing will happen in your life today that I can't handle.

The Response:

O' God, my Father and my Lord, blessings and honor are always due to you for who you are. I am grateful for the gift of another day. As I experience this day, I desire to know you better and to understand you more through your suffering and resurrection. Whatever I must go through—trials and sufferings—I pray that I may bear them as you did for me. Remind me daily that the sufferings and trials of this life are not worthy to be compared with the glory that is to come. I offer you all my heart today as a friend of Jesus sharing in His suffering. Be with me all throughout this day. Amen.

Day 104

The Reading:

Proverbs 15:33, "Fear of the Lord teaches a person to be wise; humility precedes honor."

The Revelation:

Good morning my child and may you receive all that Heaven has in store for you today and beyond. Today, I want you to understand one of the most misunderstood virtues, humility. Many people think humility is a sense of inferiority or a lack of self-appreciation. No, humility is far from this notion. True humility is an honest face of facts, admitting them and then acting according to them. To be humble means to live free of all pretense and self-deception. In true humility when others are being praised or honored you do not envy or resent them. When someone deserves honor, you applaud and celebrate with them. When they do not deserve it, you maintain an honorable and charitable silence. Likewise, when others are criticizing you, blaming you or despising you—the spirit of humility keep you undisturbed. When you are guilty of an accusation—you seek forgiveness and correct your ways. When you are innocent you maintain self control and patiently attempt to right the wrong imputed against you. I am always watching and will judge according to the facts and not what someone thinks about you. In your humility, always admit your faults and do not be afraid to practice self-appraisal when your shortcomings and limitations are identified. A truly humble person finds it hard to complain even when injustice is done to him/her. I honor those who are humble in spirit. Nothing will happen in your life today that I can't handle.

The Response:

Most gracious, loving and kind God, I honor you and praise you with much admiration and adoration. Being blessed to seek another day is a testimony of your grace and mercy. I am thankful to be alive. As I live out this day I pray that I will be simply unassuming and unpretentious. Help me to refrain and resist from putting on airs and acting superior before others. It is never my desire to make anyone feel inferior in my presence, in a spirit of humility.

When others praise me, I will thank them and thank you for empowering and endowing me to receive the success. Let me live a truthful life; a humble life and a simple life facing facts and admitting my actions. Lord, I want to be loyal to you, honored by you through my practice of true humility. Amen.

Day 105

The Reading:

1 Peter 1:13-16, "So think clearly and exercise self-control. Look forward to the special blessings that will come to you at the return of Jesus Christ. Obey God because you are his children. Don't slip back into your old ways of doing evil; you didn't know any better then. But now you must be holy in everything you do, just as God—who chose you to be his children—is holy. For he himself has said, "You must be holy because I am holy.""

The Revelation:

Good morning my child and welcome to another day ordained by God before the beginning and reserved to be a blessing for you. As you begin to grow and mature spiritually do not consider yourself holier than you were before. Your spiritual desires and progress do not consist of these alone. True spiritual progress and maturity is all about surrendering to my will. Seek to learn even more of what I think of your daily desires and life. Never think that you know enough or that you are doing well enough in your daily life. As long as I deserve better as your Lord—that what you are doing—you must never be self-satisfied. My desire for you is to gain more and more and more of my thoughts, my ways, my outlook and my desires for your life. Always seek to guide and govern your daily life according to my will for you. Receive whatever I send your way with a spirit of thanksgiving—be it success or failure, prosperity or adversity. It is all part of my plan to cultivate your holiness. As a loyal disciple always follow me in humility and in obedience. Let your patience keep you from discouragement and your love preserves you from disgust. You will then find your self advancing more toward holy perfection and pleasing me in all your ways. Come and follow me my child down the path of true holiness and nothing will happen in your life today that I can't handle.

The Response:

Oh Lord, my God—you who are perfect and holy in all your ways, I greet you this morning with thanksgiving in my heart for another day's journey. Truly, you are a God of goodness and mercy. In your word, you said, "I must be holy as you are holy", and today that is my adamant desire. As I live out this day show me and teach me how to imitate and model your holiness. It is my desire to live like Jesus, walk like Jesus, love like Jesus, forgive like Jesus and if need be suffer like Jesus. I will expose myself to His model of holiness by reading and meditating upon your word. I want to live a life of holiness worthy of your grace and favor. You have done so much for me—now help me do more for you. I truly want to live holy and pleasing in your sight. Amen.

The Reflection: [What I heard the Holy Spirit speaking into my spirit during the past seven days and how it changed me or challenged me].

_____

_____

_____

_____

_____

_____

_____

_____

_____

_____

_____

_____

_____

_____

_____

_____

_____

Day 106

The Reading:

Philippians 3:12-14 "I don't mean to say that I have already achieved these things or that I have already reached perfection! But I keep working toward that day when I will finally be all that Christ Jesus saved me for and wants me to be. No, dear brothers and sisters, I am still not all I should be,] but I am focusing all my energies on this one thing: Forgetting the past and looking forward to what lies ahead, I strain to reach the end of the race and receive the prize for which God, through Christ Jesus, is calling us up to heaven."

The Revelation:

God morning my child and may the peace and power of heaven be yours throughout this day. I do not want you to lose the hope or give up on making spiritual progress. There is still time to get into the right discipline and holy habit. If you begin now and stay focused you will notice your own growth and development. Don't put it off until tomorrow or the next day. Now is the time to dig in and do it. I want you to begin this very moment with a new daily discipline of study, prayer and meditation. At first, it may seem like a major task and struggle but, always keep the hope of succeeding towards your goal. Do not let your failures discourage you and also beware of being over-confidence, so that you may not become a victim of pride and laziness. Whenever the time comes for you to omit or forego your daily discipline of prayer and study because of some other urgent matter; when the time permits try to make it up immediately. Never let weariness cause you to skip your discipline; this can develop into a bad habit and eventually hurt you. By my grace when you fail, you can easily start again. All you have to do is: (1) Evaluate your life, (2) confront what needs to be done, (3) pray for strength and (4) begin doing it. In this life you will stumble and fail but forget it, get up and keep on trying and soon you will reach the goal. Nothing will happen in your life today that I can't handle.

The Response:

Most gracious Lord and God of life; I am thankful for this, another day. I am blessed to be alive to see another God ordained day. As I set out to live this day, help me t live each moment as you desire. If it is your will for my life, I can do whatever has been scheduled for me. Whatever your will is let me not be a coward and run from it. Help me to do my best on this day. I know I will not accomplish it all over night, but when failure comes help me to shake it off and keep pressing on. My love for you will keep me determined. Holiness is my objective and heaven is my goal. I'm on the right road now—and I refuse to look back. Amen

Day 107

The Reading:

Hebrews 12:1-2, "Therefore, since we are surrounded by such a huge crowd of witnesses to the life of faith, let us strip off every weight that slows us down, especially the sin that so easily hinders our progress. And let us run with endurance the race that God has set before us. We do this by keeping our eyes on Jesus, on whom our faith depends from start to finish.[a] He was willing to die a shameful death on the cross because of the joy he knew would be his afterward. Now he is seated in the place of highest honor beside God's throne in heaven."

The Revelation:

Good morning my child and welcome to another day of ordained life. Never let anything hinder you from making spiritual progress. Those who have risen to spiritual heights are those who have fought against whatever tried to hold them back from me. No matter how hard or difficult or disagreeable the struggle never let it weigh you down. The more you struggle and fight against your potential hindrances the more of my grace I will grant you. The more you keep trying the more I will strengthen and sustain you. Different believers will confront and face different struggles. No two persons will fight the same battles. Nevertheless, those who are most diligent and zealous will fight with fervor and make much progress even though they fight different battles than others. There will be those with fewer battles and yet not overcome them or advance in holiness. But you are to remain strong and resilient against any and all forces that seek to oppress and oppose your spiritual progress. I am always near to assist you and guide you through all of your struggles. I even know what you are capable of handling before it comes. All of you struggles are meant for your good when I permit them. As you resist them and remain faithful, you will grow stronger and your battles will become less difficult. Nothing will happen in your life today that I can't handle.

The Response:

Most gracious Lord and Redeemer, thank you for allowing me to see and live another day. I am truly blessed. I pray as I experience this day that you will teach me the strengthen me to resist and handle all hindrances that may come to oppress me. Grant me the grace to take whatever steps necessary to purify my walk with you. It is my desire to run my daily race faithfully and focused. I love you Lord and I want to please you in all that I do. May my life always reflect the life of Jesus Christ. Amen

Day 108

The Reading:

1 Corinthians 6:2-3, "Don't you know that someday we Christians are going to judge the world? And since you are going to judge the world, can't you decide these little things among yourselves? Don't you realize that we Christians will judge angels? So you should surely be able to resolve ordinary disagreements here on earth."

The Revelation:

Good morning my child and may the blessings of heaven flood your life today all day. Today, I would have you to understand without doubt that those who are loyal to my commandments in this life will not face my wrath on the Day of Judgment. When the sign of the cross appears in the sky is when I will come to judge the world. At that time all of my disciples and followers of the cross will be gathered to be with me. When that day is a reality, those who have lived holy and just will judge those who tormented and persecuted them. Those of you who humbly submit to the suffering of their foes will rise to judge even angels on that day. The humble and poor will rejoice with great confidence but the proud and selfish lovers of the world will be terrified and rightfully so. In that very hour all will see that those who chose to follow me and live holy will inherit eternal peace and bliss. Never fret because of your present suffering and persecutors. The day is coming when they will see you reigning with me in judgment. All wrongdoing will be silenced, ceased and condemned while every suffering endured with long suffering will reap joy and gladness. The unsaved will be sad with deep regret. At that time you will thank me for your hardships and trials. Your reward will be eternal and the evildoer's judgment will be final. Nothing will happen in your life today that I can't handle.

The Response:

Most gracious Lord and Comforter of my soul, I thank you and I love you for this, another day. I didn't earn it nor do I deserve it but yet you blessed me with it. I am eternally grateful. I pray that I will live this day in a way that honors your blessing and glorifies your name. I want to be found worthy of reigning with you when the Day of Judgment comes. If I shall fall short in any way please show me and teach me how to live and represent your holiness. If I am loyal to your word I need not fear your wrath or your judgment after this life. Amen

Day 109

The Reading:

2 Corinthians 5:10 "For we must all stand before Christ to be judged. We will each receive whatever we deserve for the good or evil we have done in our bodies."

The Revelation:

Good morning my child and may the favor of Heaven fulfill all of your desires today. The most undebatable thing in this life is death. Each and every person on the planet is going to die at least one time. However, death is not the very last event a person is going to experience. Even after we die there is at least one more act to be done and that is judgment. Your judgment will depend on how holy you live your earthly life. If you live honestly and holy, your reward will be Heaven. On the other hand if you live unholy and with total disregard for my commandments you will be condemned to Hell. Death, judgment, Heaven, and Hell are the four final things that each individual are moving toward each and every waking hour. If you love My Father and have faith in me—you will have nothing to fear. As long as you keep this before you in your thinking you will govern your life with holiness. Always strive to be eternity minded and you will prohibit your actions from becoming unholy. Nothing will happen in your life today that I can't handle.

The Response:

Oh Lord, my God and my Savior—I thank you for blessing me with this gift of a new day. You have truly sustained me by your grace and I am grateful. I know that death is a very present reality for all in this life. I pray that my life represents your holiness and that at the end of life's journey my soul is worthy of Heaven. I desire to live in such a way that if I die at any moment I will be ushered into your presence. Teach me to fear sin and your judgment more than death or any other earthly suffering. Amen

Day 110

The Reading:

Philippians 4:6-7 "Don't worry about anything; instead, pray about everything. Tell God what you need, and thank him for all he has done. If you do this, you will experience God's peace, which is far more wonderful than the human mind can understand. His peace will guard your hearts and minds as you live in Christ Jesus."

The Revelation:

Good morning my child and may the peace of Heaven comfort you throughout this day. All of my followers who have come and gone before you, lived in this world without grumbling or complaining. They were aware of their shortcomings and they offered up their daily struggles in reparation for their sins. Yet, they lived in peace because they kept their eyes fixed and focused on me. My child, if you want to enjoy the gift of eternal peace, you must learn how to control yourself in many things. Yes, I want you to always strive to do your best but do it solely for me. Let your loyalty always be for me and nothing else. In your service for the Kingdom, don't always expect a reward for your goodness. I have already given you more than you can ever repay me. If you feel you cannot minister to others as they deal with their faults then just mind your own business. Leave them to the path of life they have chosen. You should never lose your peace of soul because others refuse to comply with my commandments. Your first obligation is to keep peace within yourself. Then you can see how to help others obtain that peace. A peaceful person has more influence than some one who is merely learned. People are always impressed by the person who has peace. Never desire anything more or less than my will and my perfect peace will be your constant companion. Nothing will happen in your life today that I can't handle.

The Response:

O' Lord my God, how great and gracious thou art. You have kept me again through the night and have blessed me with another grand and wonderful day. I am grateful. Lord, I ask that you will help me to keep my mind at perfect peace. I pray that you will grant me the grace to seek your will and your way that I may acquire that peace that every soul craves. As I obtain your peace it is my desire to transfer that peace to those around me daily. Your sanctified will is my first concern in everything that occurs in my life today. May I be known as one of your faithful followers that attains your Heavenly peace daily. Amen.

Day 111

The Reading:

Proverbs 24:15-16 "Do not lie in wait like an outlaw at the home of the godly. And don't raid the house where the godly live. They may trip seven times, but each time they will rise again. But one calamity is enough to lay the wicked low."

The Revelation:

Good morning my child; and may the peace and joy of Heaven be your companion all day. As you receive this new day, I do not want you to be afraid nor become discouraged regarding my instructions about the way to perfection and holiness. I want you to pray for a burning desire to follow me always, make it your daily effort to keep striving. Please do not become like most who started out following me but soon yielded to the first sign of difficulty. Those who are truly and sincerely committed try again and again in spite of their repeated failures. By their refusal to quit and give up they go on to perfection. I want you to make this your daily resolution no matter how many times you fall you will keep getting up and you will keep going. Never judge your progress by your feelings or by visible signs. Just keep your intentions pure and concentrate on my teachings and you will succeed. Remember, true perfection and holiness is not achieved in a day. However, you will never acquire it if you don't start trying. No, it is not an easy thing to live loyal for me. But as long as you are putting forth an effort, I will always be there with you to guide you and to strengthen you in every way. Never become discouraged with your failures. As long as you are willing to keep trying and striving after you fail, I will be pleased and content with you. Nothing will happen in your life today that I can't handle.

The Response:

O' Lord, my God and my provider; thank you for watching over me while I slept last evening and then waking me up this morning to meet and greet the gift of another blessed day. Today is the day that I desire to keep busy and stay focused on striving for spiritual perfection. I know that it won't happen in a day nor will it be easy but, I submit to whatever is necessary to achieve this holy objective. I ask that you grant me the grace to look beyond my failures and faults and not let them discourage me. I pray that you will strengthen my determination to live for you and model the perfection of Jesus Christ. As I continue to practice the acts of holiness. I know I will grow and grow closer to you in spiritual perfection. I pray that I will keep trying daily. Amen

Day 112

The Reading:

Psalm 37:23-24, "The steps of the godly are directed by the Lord. He delights in every detail of their lives. Though they stumble, they will not fall, for the Lord holds them by the hand."

The Revelation:

Good morning my child and blessings be unto you from my Father in Heaven. We have already shared with you in the past that where there is order, there you will find peace. My peace does not leave you until some disorder comes into your soul. This disorder can be anything from your thinking to your behavior. Whatever is in your life that is not in line with my word is disorder. There are many in this life, either through ignorance or neglect, who fail to see life's daily events my way. Many people are troubled, many are anxious, many are disturbed and many are ready to do anything for some need or advantage in their earthly life. Whenever you have doubts regarding which way to take always consult my word or me and I will order your steps. Never take your eye off of my ways and teachings. Otherwise, the enemy can easily deceive you. Let no human accolade or praise influence you to drift from my holy path. When you follow me and submit to my direction your feet will be firm and you will have peace. Always remain wise in this matter. Do not have any arbitrary desires. Place all of your hopes, your plans and your efforts at my feet. Always follow that which is wise and holy but never pursue that which is opposed to my will no matter what the price. When you follow your own selfish desires you will only find regrets and remorse. There is only one way to lasting peace and that is my will and my way. Nothing will happen in your life today that I can't handle.

The Response:

Most kind and loving God, I greet you with gratitude and thanksgiving in my heart for another day in this life. As I start out this day, you know what is best for me. I know everything that you allow to happen in my life today is good for me in some way. Even though I may not understand the way you have prepared for me to take I will gladly and humbly yield to it. Lord, I ask that you will order each of my steps throughout this day and lead me where you will have me to go. You know what and where is best for me. My highest wisdom lies in embracing your will for my life. I only want to go and do what you want for me. Amen

The Reflection: [What I heard the Holy Spirit speaking into my spirit during the past seven days and how it changed me or challenged me].

_____

_____

_____

_____

_____

_____

_____

_____

_____

_____

_____

_____

_____

_____

_____

_____

Day 113

The Reading:

2 Timothy 2:11-13, "This is a true saying: If we die with him, we will also live with him. If we endure hardship, we will reign with him. If we deny him, he will deny us. If we are unfaithful, he remains faithful, for he cannot deny himself."

The Revelation:

Good morning my child, and may this day be full of blessings and favor like you have never experienced before. As you set out on your journey for this day, please do not let yourself become crushed by the various activities you will engage in. Nothing you do, especially for the sake of my kingdom, should sadden you or burden your spirit. What you do for the kingdom and me should advance you spiritually beyond your fondest hopes and dreams. The hardships and trials that confront you daily in this life are rapidly passing away. You need to know that the longest life on this earth is brief. Only eternity is unending. If you will bear and endure your trials, troubles and tribulations with patience and faith, I will send relief for you as soon as you have benefited from the experience. Whatever you are called upon to endure and encounter while you are on earth is only minute and a small price to pay for the blessings you will receive in Heaven. When heaven is finally your home, you will then see how Paul's words were true when he said the sufferings of this present age is nothing compared with the glory to come. Submit and surrender yourself completely in my hands. Always bring your joys and your sorrows to me. Make me your closest and best friend. You will find your hardships easy to endure when you let me lead and guide you. Fix and focus more on me and less on your trials. Nothing will happen in your life today that I can't handle.

The Response:

O' Lord, how excellent is your name, and how perfect is your love in all the earth. Thank you for another day in this life. As this day unfolds before me teach me to rely completely on you and to stay focused on your will. Help me to realize that from time to time some of my trials are good for me. In my trials teach me to lean and depend on you and to stick to your plan for my life. Lord, you deserve my complete allegiance and loyalty for what you have already endured and done for all. As I go through this life—make me mindful that the night is quickly forgotten when morning comes. As I go through the darkness of this life—help me to endure it and look beyond it toward Heaven. Amen

Day 114

The Reading:

John 12:25-26, "Those who love their life in this world will lose it. Those who despise their life in this world will keep it for eternal life. All those who want to be my disciples must come and follow me, because my servants must be where I am. And if they follow me, the Father will honor them."

The Revelation:

Good morning my child and welcome to the favor of my Father through another blessed day. There are so many people who deceive themselves through life. They think they are living a good life simply because they perform a few earthly tasks. Some even go to church once or twice a week, sing a song and say a prayer and think they are holy before me, because they commit no public crimes. Yet, I am still displeased with them because daily they lived as though they depend on no one but themselves. Many of them are too interested in following their own interests and own ways. No, they do not deny my wisdom in theory but they disregard it in practice. But you my child, I want you to follow my words daily and when you do many of your daily difficulties will cease being problems. I don't want you to be afraid of applying my word to your everyday life. Don't be afraid of losing some worldly advantage or engagement. Remember, many people are trying to get to Heaven with little suffering as possible. These people work and sweat only for their earthly desires. Their only pay check is their fear of Hell and not their genuine love for me. I will not have you worrying your way through this life. You are very dear to me and I am very interested in you. When you follow me; when you serve me you will never have to fear or fall prey to confusion because my power and presence are always near and available to you. Your daily life will prove to me how loyal you are in the faith and how much you love me. Don't be deceived, I am always watching. Nothing will happen in your life today that I can't handle.

The Response:

Most gracious Lord and King of all, I greet you with thanksgiving in my heart and I shout Hallelujah for this a brand new and blessed day. Your wisdom, power and love have again manifested themselves before me and I am eternally grateful. As I live out this day I want to prove with my life that I love you and believe in you and trust you above anybody and anything else. Teach me more about your word and your wisdom that I may appreciate it better. I want to follow you and serve you with my whole heart. I never want to deceive myself into thinking that I am all that without you. I love you Lord and I pray that my life will prove it today. Amen

Day 115

The Reading:

Luke 6:37-38, "Stop judging others, and you will not be judged. Stop criticizing others, or it will all come back on you. If you forgive others, you will be forgiven. If you give, you will receive. Your gift will return to you in full measure, pressed down, shaken together to make room for more, and running over. Whatever measure you use in giving—large or small—it will be used to measure what is given back to you." Stop judging others, and you will not be judged. Stop criticizing others, or it will all come back on you. If you forgive others, you will be forgiven. If you give, you will receive. Your gift will return to you in full measure, pressed down, shaken together to make room for more, and running over. Whatever measure you use in giving—large or small—it will be used to measure what is given back to you."

The Revelation:

Good morning my child and may the glory of Heaven shine down on you as the noon day sun. As you continue to grow in this relationship always remember the lesson which I modeled with my life and teachings on earth. All greatness is but a shadow or an image of uncreated greatness. Man or woman in and of himself or herself is nothing without me. However, if they follow my words, they will share in my glory in Heaven. The lesson is this—never think so much of yourself when you know you are made from nothing; always exhibit and example humility. Do not let your pride and vanity show. How can you find faults with others when you yourself are so possessed with faults? Without my grace and help you, too, will yield and fall prey to the same temptations you judge others for. Unless it is your spiritual duty to correct others, give attention to your own faults and not to others. As you work to contain and correct your own shortcomings you will be too busy to see them in others. The best knowledge you could ever acquire is to know my will for your life and seek ways to rid yourself of sins. No matter how holy you may think you are, you will fall short. It is my desire for you to esteem and edify others more than to criticize and condemn them. Nothing will happen in your life today that I can't handle.

The Response:

Most gracious and forgiving God, I salute you this morning with praise and thanksgiving. I honor you with words of adoration and appreciation for blessing me to see another day. As I live out the hours of this day, help me to never pretend to be more than I am. Teach me not to judge others for their faults when I am just as plagued with my own faults. I desire a healthy and holy love for others to grow in your grace. Teach me how not to be a faultfinder but a model of your mercy. I love you Lord and I want to be to others what you are to me. Amen

Day 116

The Reading:

Philippians 2:12-13, "Dearest friends, you were always so careful to follow my instructions when I was with you. And now that I am away you must be even more careful to put into action God's saving work in your lives, obeying God with deep reverence and fear. For God is working in you, giving you the desire to obey him and the power to do what pleases him."

The Revelation:

Good morning my child and welcome to another pre-ordained and consecrated day. May this day continue to reveal the love of God and the joy of Heaven to you. As you journey throughout this day, mind your own business and do not present yourself as a judge before those around you. There is a lot that you do not know about your neighbor. This makes it hard to pass judgment on others as they may deserve. Be wise and prudent and leave all judgment to me. It is far more wiser to evaluate and judge yourself. Greater good can be done by judging yourself and correcting your own faults than by pointing out others faults. The best and most profitable thing you can do for others is set a good example and say a sincere prayer for them. People will come to annoy you because you don't mind your own business or because you lack understanding in their matters. Most people are not at fault when they get on your last nerve. The real issue is within you. When you focus on your own faults and get busy trying to deal with those faults, you will immediately discover you don't have enough time to become annoyed by other people issues. Just think about how much peace of soul you can enjoy if you would learn to mind your own business and work out your own salvation. Most of the time you are wrong anyway when you judge others. If the truth be told, you are only aroused against others when they oppose your pride or selfishness. Never expect everybody to see things your way. Every person is different and each person has his/her own tastes and experiences. Those whom you condemned are often excused by Heaven. Handle your own affairs and faults and leave the judging to me. Nothing will happen in your life today that I can't handle.

The Response:

O' Lord my God, the only fair and perfect judge. Honor and glory be unto you for another blessed day. Thank you for your grace and mercy. I pray for heavenly wisdom so that I may not be unreasonable in my judgments and opinions of others. Just as you treat each person as individuals, I desire to be like you in the way I treat other people. Let me not judge those who do not do things my way. I pray I will spend more time and pay more attention working on my own faults than those of my neighbors. When I cannot say anything good about others help me to keep silent. Amen

Day 117

The Reading:

Ecclesiastes 11:7-9, "Light is sweet; it's wonderful to see the sun! When people live to be very old, let them rejoice in every day of life. But let them also remember that the dark days will be many. Everything still to come is meaningless. Young man, it's wonderful to be young! Enjoy every minute of it. Do everything you want to do; take it all in. But remember that you must give an account to God for everything you do."

The Revelation:

Good morning my child and welcome to another wonderful and blessed day under the sun. I know there are times in your spirit when you feel that your earthly life would be much easier and better if you could do your own thing and follow your own ways. You notice worldly people and conclude that they are enjoying life without having to submit to me. Don't be deceived; their life is not all that it seems. True, they may be following after their own pleasure for a season but very soon they are bound to reflect on the brevity of life and the passing of earthly satisfaction. When any one forgets me, they will look back and see all of the pleasures and joys of this world have come to an end. They will never again look forward to any kind of happiness. Don't be deceived; even those who seem to be enjoying the pleasures of this world have their share of worries, fears and bitterness. They, too, know the meaning of disappointment and failure. Just as smoke disappears quickly in the air, so too will this earth and its pleasures. It is also worthy to note that many earthly pleasures cease pleasing people long before they are lost. What was supposed to bring happiness often times bring sorrow and disappointment. There have been many prominent people whose days ended in bitterness. I want you, my child, to cling to my righteousness and me and embrace the only true and lasting joy—Heaven. Nothing will happen in your life today that I can't handle.

The Response:

O Lord, my God and my salvation, thanks be unto you for blessing me to see another day. As I embrace this gift of life, I pray that I will not become enticed by the pleasures of this world. I know you do not forbid me to enjoy this life as long as I do not seek after that which is wrong and unworthy of human dignity. I do not wish to risk gaining Heaven for anything or anybody. My hope is in your help to keep me focus on Heaven and not the passing pleasures of this world. Amen.

Day 118

The Reading:

Romans 12:3, "As God's messenger, I give each of you this warning: Be honest in your estimate of yourselves, measuring your value by how much faith God has given you."

The Revelation:

Good morning my child and may the blessings of Heaven surround you all day. I want you to be very cautious of becoming over confidence in yourself. This kind of pride can hurt you badly. Never be satisfied with yourself but strive to become better and better everyday. The only person who is safe from sinking in serious sin is the person who fears and avoids it. If it wasn't for my grace you would succumb to sin because of your weakness. Never take chances with sin; always avoid every occasion of sin at all cost. Whether it be a person, place or thing shun it. Always remember the person that loves danger shall perish in it. When you gamble with your soul only you are at stake. You will be lost forever if you die in your sin. The very thought of losing Heaven should terrify you. Thus, never let pride intoxicate you in thinking you are more than what you are. That's the first step towards Hell. My Father is kind in every way but He cannot and will not tolerate presumption and pride. This is why the saints of old refused to take chances with temptations and sin in their day. The reward, which my Father offers, was and is too wonderful and grand to forfeit. Never think more of yourself, my child, than what you truly are. My Father honors and exalts the humble but the proud He detests. Always be mindful of this, you are what you are because of Heaven's grace and mercy. Nothing will happen in your life today that I can't handle.

The Response:

God of mercy and God of love—I greet you and I honor you with thanksgiving and praise in my heart. You have been more than merciful to me. Allowing me to witness another day is proof of your undying love for my life. As I am being thankful today for your grace, I do not want to presume anything of myself. I am here and blessed all because of you. Keep me mindful of my limitations and my proclivity to sin. If it wasn't for you strengthening me,

I couldn't resist the temptation sin. Teach me to walk humbly and to avoid every occasion to sin. I know my only security from Hell is a life of continual effort against my faults and weaknesses. Continue to lead and guide me with your love. Amen.

Day 119

The Reading:

Psalm 62:8, "O my people, trust in him at all times. Pour out your heart to him, for God is our refuge."

The Revelation:

Good morning my child and may the peace of eternity be your constant companion today. There is nothing on this earth that doesn't need my support in order to exist. If I withdrew myself for one single second every thing would vanish like a vapor into nothing. It is I, your Lord, who provide for all things from the moment they begin to have their being in order for them to fulfill their purpose. My child, I am the fountain of all that is good; I am the power behind all that has life and I am the depth of all wisdom and knowledge. When you put your unyielding trust in me—it will become your highest wisdom and your deepest consolation. The more you seek consolation anywhere else, the more you will discover how limited, brief and imperfect it is. When you learn to place your trust and confidence in me alone and at all times—you will enjoy the peace of a pure heart. I don't want you to merely talk to me as your hope but prove your sincerity and love by a steadfast trust in my words and wisdom, no matter what happens in your daily life. Always prove your trust in me by setting no limitations and putting no conditions or reservations on our relationship. I want you to want what I want for you. Desire my decisions for you in everything and I will send only that which is best for you. Always trust in me and believe that I will not allow you to suffer anything, which is not good for you in the end. Nothing will happen in your life today that I can't handle.

The Response:

God of mercy and God of love—I lift your name with the highest praise for who you are. I also thank you with a perpetual praise for waking me up this morning and starting me on my way. I am truly blessed! I place my trust and my life completely in your hands. I submit all of my cares, my sorrows, my labors and my fears to you. I will always trust you above anything or any body else. I ask that you guide my thoughts and actions this day and every day of my earthly life. I desire to follow your holy will as it comes to me in all circumstances. I will trust in you always. Amen.

The Reflection: [What I heard the Holy Spirit speaking into my spirit during the past seven days and how it changed me or challenged me].

_____

_____

_____

_____

_____

_____

_____

_____

_____

_____

_____

_____

_____

_____

_____

_____

_____

Day 120

The Reading:

1 John 2:15-17 "Stop loving this evil world and all that it offers you, for when you love the world, you show that you do not have the love of the Father in you. For the world offers only the lust for physical pleasure, the lust for everything we see, and pride in our possessions. These are not from the Father. They are from this evil world. And this world is fading away, along with everything it craves. But if you do the will of God, you will live forever."

The Revelation:

Good morning my child and may the riches of Heaven fall down upon you throughout the day. I want you to be aware of the spirit of worldliness. This spirit can easily blind you to the truth, make you think more of this world than of the eternal world to come. The spirit of worldliness can deceive you so that you will be ready and willing to toil for death than to strive and struggle for life. When you become intoxicated by the spirit of worldliness; you will yearn more for appearing great then actually being great in character, integrity and in living a holy life. If you would take some time to examine those who think and invent more in this life you would quickly learn how foolish they are for loving it too much. The world you are in is full of so much pain, persecution and problems. So much so that many people often find bitterness where they had hoped for sweetness. True happiness and peace that so many long for can never be attain in this world. Do not let appearances fool you. Those who are addicted to this world is doomed to disappointment. You will never be dismayed or disappointed as long as you submit to my will. Do not love this world or the things in the world. Always keep your trust in me and I will forever bless you. Nothing will happen in your life today that I can't handle.

The Response:

My Lord and my God, I am eternally grateful for another day in this life. Once again you have extended your grace to me and I am forever thankful. As I live out this day help me not to put my trust in this world or the things of this world. They are both fading away. My desire is for those things that are holy and eternal. Take away from me whatever may entice me to attach myself to this world. I long for the joy and happiness of Heaven. I pray for bitterness against anything that seeks to hinder me from inheriting my place with you. Amen.

Day 121

The Reading:

Romans 8:9-10 "But you are not controlled by your sinful nature. You are controlled by the Spirit if you have the Spirit of God living in you. (And remember that those who do not have the Spirit of Christ living in them are not Christians at all.) Since Christ lives within you, even though your body will die because of sin, your spirit is alive because you have been made right with God."

The Revelation:

Good morning my child and may the favor of God testify to His love and grace in your life. As long as you have the sanctifying grace of he Holy Spirit within your soul, I will be in constant fellowship with you no matter what. The more you are aware of this fellowship the more your life will be influenced by my Holiness. It is my desire that you will live a daily life of active holiness in order to gain the full benefit of our friendship and fellowship. Through the various means of prayer and Bible reading learn to tune your mind into me often throughout the day. When you are operating in the spirit, you will remain centered on my perfection and power. In doing this, your inner peace will not become disturbed by that or those who are around you daily. Our daily fellowship, prompt by the presence of the Holy Spirit, is just the beginning of eternal peace and joy that awaits you in Heaven. You will easily recognize my joy because you are in a right relationship with me. You will easily recognize my peace because you submit to my will. When you abide in a right and Holy fellowship with me, your life will become a reflection of me and my spirit will be obvious in your life. This fellowship is only strengthen when you spend quality holy time in prayer and study. These holy habits will also keep you aware of my very present help to share your burdens and encourage your faith. Strive daily to perfect your fellowship with me. Nothing will happen in your life today that I can't handle.

The Response:

O' Lord my God, the author and finisher of my faith; the keeper of my soul—I love you and I am grateful to you for another day's journey. You have kept me and blessed me with the gift of another day. You have proven your love for me and now I desire to prove my love and loyalty to you. Teach me how to strengthen my fellowship with you through prayer and reading your word daily. As I live out this day let me give you more of myself through my thoughts, words and deeds. I yearn to live each day of my life in perfect fellowship with you until I am able to live it eternally when this life is over. Bless me and keep me. Amen.

Day 122

The Reading:

Luke 14:18, "For the proud will be humbled, but the humble will be honored."

The Revelation:

Good morning my child and may the blessings of Heaven rain down upon you like perpetual rain drops. As you continue to humble yourself and avoid all forms of admiration, praise and honor, you will continue to yield yourself more and more to my will. Your desire to remain humble will foster a spirit of obeying than commanding; serving rather than being served, praising rather than being praised. In your own way you will seek to match my generosity with gratitude. Your spirit of humility and self-abasement will facilitate all of this. On the other hand, your humility should not hinder you from doing your best daily for the kingdom. Remember, I practiced the same humility through my daily life from the cradle to the cross. Please know no matter how much you humble yourself, you will never equal my life and death. However, I still want you to imitate me through your spirit of humility. Never give too much thought to being despised and mistreated in this life. Forget the fear of ridicule and contempt, which you suffer for my namesake and give no thought to the advancing of the wicked agenda. Soon and very soon you are going to be impressed by my eternal greatness and goodness when you inherit heaven. Remain holy and humble and always know, nothing will happen in your life today that I can't handle.

The Response:

O' Lord, my Lord how excellent is thy name and thy example in all the earth. I thank you for this day. I thank you for your mercy. I thank you for your on going fellowship in my life. I pray today that I may continue to practice holiness and humility in my determination to serve you without pride or self-deception. I ask that you would flood my mind with your example of humility and my will to satisfy you even through suffering. Teach me to empty myself of self-love through self-abasement for the love of you and Heaven. Amen.

Day 123

The Reading:

1 Corinthians 1:20-21, "So where does this leave the philosophers, the scholars, and the world's brilliant debaters? God has made them all look foolish and has shown their wisdom to be useless nonsense. Since God in his wisdom saw to it that the world would never find him through human wisdom, he has used our foolish preaching to save all who believe."

The Revelation:

Good morning my child and may you receive this day with the joy in which it was created. Today, I want you to understand that this is an eternal different between a person who learns by natural talent and the person who learns by my grace. All knowledge, which comes by my grace, is far higher than any knowledge that is gained by any other means. The wisdom and knowledge that is gained by grace brings a holy joy to your soul and renews the energy of life for your daily walk. Worldly wisdom is foolishness composed to heavenly wisdom. My wisdom teaches the freedom of self-control, humility and the joy of spiritual perfection. The world is always fascinated by the deeds of those who are selfish. The world envies those who are rich, attractive, clever, strong and smart. The wise person admires and imitates the one who is prayerful and patent. The unselfish person is often frowned upon and considered foolish. People of the world who call themselves wise judge greatness by external appearances and achievements. I judge from Heaven first and foremost what is in a person's heart more so than what is in a person's head. Never forget the greatest knowledge in the world in the entire universe is the knowledge of God's love. The bedrock of truly and Godly wisdom is the fear or reverence of my Father. Let this knowledge be your guiding light to the fountain of eternal wisdom. Nothing will happen in your life today that I can't handle.

The Response:

Most gracious, loving and all knowing God, thank you for watching over me last night, thank you for waking me up this morning. Thank you for being merciful and blessing me to see another day. As this day begins, I pray for eternal wisdom to live out this day in union with your will. Teach me your way in the midst of this dark and confused world. Let the light of your truth shine bright on my spirit so that I may know the way. I submit to the teachings of your word and your holy spirit. I yearn to learn your way and none other. Amen.

Day 124

The Reading:

Romans 6:12-14, "Do not let sin control the way you live; do not give in to its lustful desires. Do not let any part of your body become a tool of wickedness, to be used for sinning. Instead, give yourselves completely to God since you have been given new life. And use your whole body as a tool to do what is right for the glory of God. Sin is no longer your master, for you are no longer subject to the law, which enslaves you to sin. Instead, you are free by God's grace."

The Revelation:

Good morning my child and may the grace and goodness of God be evident at every turn you make today. As you reflect upon heaven's grace today, please know that this is not some holy feeling or mood you are experiencing. This is an intelligent effort on our part to be in a right fellowship with me. Your desire for holy devotion is a great gift of grace. And as long as you make a sincere effort to turn your back on anything that attempts to hinder your spiritual progress I will grant you more of this grace. You must continuously empty yourself of all useless interests in order to make room for my will. More than often-it is the small things that prevent my saints from obtaining this grace. I desire you to have as much of my grace as you want. Why? Because it will make you loyal to me in all things. If you have not obtained this grace yet it because you have not prepared your soul for it. I want you to pray fervently for it and labor night and day for it. Above all battle against those things in your life that blocks the flow of this grace. My child, do not forget, you are no longer under the law but grace. With this grace you are entitled to all of the privileges of Heaven. Never lose sight of the cross and its redeeming power. Because of this you no longer have to depend on feelings or moods but on my Father's grace and love. Nothing will happen in your life today that I can't handle.

The Response:

Most gracious Savoir, thank you for another day on this side of Heaven. I am forever grateful for your grace. As you continue to extend your grace to me—may I continue to express my gratitude by way of my obedience and loyalty to your holy word. I pray that I will be true to my devotion with you daily. No matter how difficult the journey—it is my desire never to take your grace for granted or displease you in any way. Help me to avoid all sin and never lose sight of the power and grace, which sustains my life. Your grace is grand! Amen.

Day 125

The Reading:

Micah 7:5-6, "Don't trust anyone—not your best friend or even your wife! For the son despises his father. The daughter defies her mother. The daughter-in-law defies her mother-in-law. Your enemies will be right in your own household."

The Revelation:

Good morning my child and welcome to another ordained and orchestrated day under Heaven. As this day continues to unfold meditate on this caution, do not put too much trust in human friendships and human relationships. While experiencing this life you will quickly learn that humans can only bring and offer limited help to your daily needs. When you depend on human help too much it will lead to bitter disappointment. Above any and every thing that you seek to satisfy your daily needs always put your main trust in me. You need to keep forever in the forefront of your mind. The people who are for you today may stand adversely against you tomorrow. The people who please you today may displease you tomorrow. The material substances that satisfy you today may dissatisfy you tomorrow. Never submit yourself to these ever changing and ever shifting creatures. No one on the planet will ever come close to fulfilling your needs and satisfying you like me. Only I am unchanging and all satisfying. Only I alone know and want what is best for you. Too many of my saints do not trust and believe in me as I desire and demand. If you would simply put your daily trust in me, I will grant you my perfect peace and you will discover Heaven's perfect life is the only lasting good for you. I will never fail you. Remember, nothing will happen in your life today that I can't handle.

The Response:

Most gracious and grand God of the entire universe, I give thanks to you for your mercy and kindness. Thank you for this gift of another day. As I live out the minutes and seconds of this day teach me how to rely on no one and no thing but you. Let me not depend on human help but on you and your Holy Spirit for my life. As I walk among mortals on this day I pray that I will keep my eyes fixed on you. Granted that I may never again misplace my trust and confidence in things that are human but solely and sincerely surrender every thing to you. Amen.

Day 126

The Reading:

2 Peter 2:19-20 "They promise freedom, but they themselves are slaves to sin and corruption. For you are a slave to whatever controls you. And when people escape from the wicked ways of the world by learning about our Lord and Savior Jesus Christ and then get tangled up with sin and become its slave again, they are worse off than before."

The Revelation:

Good morning my child, may the perfect peace and joy of Heaven be yours all throughout this day. While on your journey today I pray that you will not allow yourself to become attached to the things of this world. If you do, these things may become too strong for you and make you their slave. This will eventually cause you to submit to sin because of them. I am aware that your likes and dislikes can be concluded by an act of your will; nevertheless, you can control them through prayer, fasting and daily study of my word. Keep yourself purified from earthly attractions and attachments by yielding to my commandments. Only with a pure love for my laws will you be able to escape the enslavement of the things of this world. When you submit to my laws you will never again become too troubled about losing something—whether it is a friend or a cherished possession. Always, and I mean always choose first things first: God before any creature or created thing. My child, refuse to be a slave to anything or anybody on earth. I desire you to love me and my will more than anything else. Again, never become so attached to any human or any earthly satisfaction so much that you would sin for them. If you love anything that much you are simply a misguided fool. You should never prefer a reflection of my Father more than my Father, Himself. If you want true joy and greatness attach yourself to me. Nothing will happen in your life today that I can't handle.

The Response:

Good morning, my God and my Savior, thank you for waking me up this morning and bringing me again through the night into another marvelous day. I submit that you are the perfect God. It is my desire to attach myself to your will and your word as I live out this day. Let me love and choose only that which will help me and please you. Show me your will today and grant me the strength to follow it. Amen.

The Reflection: [What I heard the Holy Spirit speaking into my spirit during the past seven days and how it changed me or challenged me].

_____

_____

_____

_____

_____

_____

_____

_____

_____

_____

_____

_____

_____

_____

_____

_____

Day 127

The Reading:

James 1:8, "They can't make up their minds. They waver back and forth in everything they do."

The Revelation:

Good morning my child and may your day be flooded with the joys of Heaven throughout every moment. The lesson I want you to gain today is never allow yourself to become discouraged because your positive disposition for me changes so easily. One moment you may feel a burning desire to serve me and a little later you feel disconnected and uninterested in me. Do not let this instability sadden your spirit. These spiritual mood swings are a part of the process of purifying your soul. If you remain resolute about your intentions in serving me, you will grow stronger in your allegiance to me. My saints of every age experience these spiritual shifts also but they were determined to please me regardless of their moods. Feelings of devotion are a spiritual gift from me to motivate you to stay connected to me. After you make a vow to me, I may remove the feeling in order that you may prove your sincerity or insincerity. Yes, it is easy to make a vow to me when you are feeling devout and devoted but when the feelings are gone the vow usually vanishes with it. I want you to trust in me and never doubt my promises to bless you. When you continue to believe and remain faithful to my word even when the feeling or mood is good, it is then you prove yourself a true follower of mine. No one, my child is ready to see my Father face to face in Heaven, until He has proven himself worthy while on earth. One's sincerity and pure trust is tested when his/her resolve for Heaven remains strong. Learn to conquer your moods and doubting spirit by exercising your faith. Nothing will happen in your life today that I can't handle.

The Response:

O' Lord, my God I greet you with awesome wonder for the grand grace you continuously offer me. Thank you for your generous favor to allow me to see this blessed day. Whatever comes my way today—light or darkness; sorrow or joy; wealth or poverty, let me turn to you and prove my trust in you. Let my love and loyalty shine brightly through my belief and actions. My moods may change and my feelings may vary but let my will or desires follow your way. Grant me the strength to conquer my doubting spirit. Amen.

Day 128

The Reading:

2 Peter 3:17-18 "I am warning you ahead of time, dear friends, so that you can watch out and not be carried away by the errors of these wicked people. I don't want you to lose your own secure footing. But grow in the special favor and knowledge of our Lord and Savior Jesus Christ. To him be all glory and honor, both now and forevermore. Amen."

The Revelation:

Good morning my child and may you receive every blessing that come your way today with pen arms and heart. As often as time will permit you throughout this day, I would like for you to seek communion with me. You must learn to turn to me as your spiritual ancestors did in order to keep growing in my grace. When you turn to me, I will endow your mind with great thoughts, which will elevate you spiritually above an earthly level. When you seek constant communion with me, I will refresh you console you, strengthen you, make you wise and grant you heavenly joy. Be prepared to come to me for loving companionship and I will draw nearer to you with greater graces. You will be raised up to heavenly heights where you will receive a broader view of life, a deeper understanding and greater strength to handle your daily burdens. Strive daily to grow in my grace and learn to enter into all I experienced while on earth. Every thought, every word and every act that I experienced while on earth was all lived for the love of you. My life belongs to you. Please learn to grow in it and share in it through daily prayer reflection and meditation. The more you seek to grow in me and become a constant communion of mine, the more I will share your earthly life by granting you my grace. I love you and look forward to our daily fellowship as we share in each other. And remember nothing will happen in your life today that I can't handle.

The Response:

My dear Heavenly Father, thank you for keeping my life through the night. Thank you for ordaining another day and allowing me to experience it. Your faithfulness is forever true. I am filled with joy overflowing in my heart for gaining this new revelation today. I can penetrate the barriers of time and space and enter into your earthly life as you enter into mine. Today, I desire to do whatever is necessary to grow in your grace and become a constant companion of yours. I will give daily time, attention and reflection to following after your life. I only ask that you grant me the faith and love that I need to constantly give of myself to you in daily prayer. Amen.

Day 129

The Reading:

James 1:2-4 "Dear brothers and sisters, whenever trouble comes your way, let it be an opportunity for joy. For when your faith is tested, your endurance has a chance to grow. So let it grow, for when your endurance is fully developed, you will be strong in character and ready for anything."

The Revelation:

Good morning my child and may grace and mercy be your constant companion on your journey throughout this day. I want you to know that temptations are very profitable to your spiritual growth and development—even though they be troublesome and distressing. Temptations help you to lessen your foolish pride by showing you just how weak you are in certain areas of your life. Without temptations you can deceive yourself into dangerous self-confidence. Temptations can be a good teacher in many ways that will help you draw closer to me in your daily life. Temptations can purify your soul by forcing you to resist evil and practice my will. Your troubles, your afflictions and your oppositions offer you great opportunities to gain heavenly merits. You will never know your true self until you have experienced various temptations. When they come; they will help your virtues to shine out and also help you to see what spiritual progress you are making. My child, anyone can act holy and virtuous when things are going well. It's the believers who remain long suffering in the times of adversity, can rightly for hope a lasting reward in Heaven. Note, if you were never tempted, you would never discover your real self. Anyone can talk about a holy life but it is only proven through living a holy life. When temptations come your way today they are giving you a chance to prove how serious you are when you say you want to please me and live a holy daily life for me. Nothing will happen in your life today that I can't handle.

The Response:

O' Lord my God, I greet you in the spirit of thanksgiving and joy for the gift of another day. It is my desire to live this day pleasing you in every way. I desire, too, to be loyal to your word and your will. Grant me your grace to see and own my faults and to overcome them. When temptations come my way today I ask for strength and wisdom to contradict and conquer them. I would rather die today then to yield to any temptation and offend you. I love you Lord and I want to prove it with my life. Amen.

Day 130

The Reading:

Philippians 2:12-14, "Dearest friends, you were always so careful to follow my instructions when I was with you. And now that I am away you must be even more careful to put into action God's saving work in your lives, obeying God with deep reverence and fear. For God is working in you, giving you the desire to obey him and the power to do what pleases him. In everything you do, stay away from complaining and arguing."

The Revelation:

Good morning my child and may this day be one filled with new beginnings for you. As you engage this day and its many opportunities, I pray that you would begin it by taking reasonable care of yourself. If temptations should come your way in any form arouse yourself, warn yourself, guard yourself and avoid idleness. No matter how much you do for others, please don't neglect your own spiritual being. Beware of too much talking and whenever possible try to get alone with me. When possible, try to live every moment of your life in my presence. Please listen careful, if you neglect yourself, you can lose your spiritual strength, which was attained over time through prayer and discipline. Constantly reflect over our relationship and your purpose in this life. Examine your progress of self, daily. Continue to feed and nurture yourself on my word and through prayer. Do not invest spiritual energies in the affairs of others. This, too, can drain you and leave you depleted. Keep your attention fix on your own faults and try to correct them. When it comes to the affairs of others all you can do is pray for them. Do this as one sinner praying for another and leave the rest to me. When you learn this great lesson you will find great peace for your soul. Learning to mind your own business is a great virtue to acquire and maintain. Do what you can my child to help others to live a holier and happier life and submit everything else to me. Always strive to keep yourself healthy and holy. Nothing will happen in your life today that I can't handle.

The Response:

O Lord, my God and my Savior, I give thanks and praise to you on this, another blessed day. I worship you for who you are and what you are in my life. I ask you as I live out this day to bless me with the courage to examine myself; the honesty to admit my own faults and limitations; the sincerity to seek self-improvement and the love and loyalty for you to keep me striving for perfection the rest of my life. Help me not to be concerned about the matters that are out of my control, except to intercede and to petition you through prayer. Let my life become the epitome and the example of the words, "Thy will be done." Amen.

Day 131

The Reading:

Matthew 26:40-42, "Then he returned to the disciples and found them asleep. He said to Peter, "Couldn't you stay awake and watch with me even one hour? Keep alert and pray. Otherwise temptation will overpower you. For though the spirit is willing enough, the body is weak! Again he left them and prayed, "My Father! If this cup cannot be taken away until I drink it, your will be done.""

The Revelation:

Good morning my child and may the graces of Heaven surround you all day. As you take time for daily meditation today, reflect upon the saints of old and learn how they willingly submitted to my will with undying fervor. This kind of fervor is not about a matter of feelings or moods but it is all about an unconditional attachment to my will. At this moment in your life, can you say with honesty that you are living a life that compares to the unselfishness of the saints of old? They were so loyal to me that they were unable to say "No" to me, no matter what I asked of them. Whether it was sickness, hard work, failures, persecution or criticisms they always strived to do their best in pleasing me. I want you to practice every day imitating their loyalty to my will and me. When you do, you will receive heavenly peace of the soul. Your daily tasks will seem less of a burden because I will send you my grace to strengthen and encourage you. My fervent followers are always eager to know my will in the events of their lives. Even though their feelings and moods may change from time to time their fervor remained the same, to please me. As you continue to grow spiritually you will come to know that your greatest satisfaction on earth will only come from submitting and following my will. Please never stop trying to live each day, as I desire. Remember, nothing will happen in your life today that I can't handle.

The Response:

My God and my joy, I greet you with much humility and praise in my heart for sparing me to see another day and for granting me another opportunity to please you. Thank you, too, for showing me—one of the reasons I make so many mistakes is because I don't take the time to learn what your will is. I know time is short and I don't want to waste any more of it with half-heartedness. Teach me your will and show me how to follow it. You desire action and I want to please you. Today, I am willing to submit to your perfect will in my thinking, in my speaking and in my acting. Amen.

Day 132

The Reading:

Colossians 1:27-28, "For it has pleased God to tell his people that the riches and glory of Christ are for you Gentiles, too. For this is the secret: Christ lives in you, and this is your assurance that you will share in his glory. So everywhere we go, we tell everyone about Christ. We warn them and teach them with all the wisdom God has given us, for we want to present them to God, perfect in their relationship to Christ."

The Revelation:

Good morning my child and welcome to this blessed day. I pray that you will receive and honor it as a special gift of life. As long as you are on earth, you will need food, medicine, rest, water, companionship and recreation to survive. Nevertheless, I do not want you to make the mistake of considering these natural things as the only remedies to sustain your life. If you do, you will place too much hope and value in them. This will cause you to expect more from them than they can possibly give you. It is only from me that you can even begin to expect divine happiness and peace. If you would be wise you would place your hope in me and me alone. I am the creator and preserver of all things. Nothing or no one can help you if I do not ordain it with the power to do so. When you place your hope in me above everybody and everything, you will never be disappointed. I will never let you down. My child, please do not place too much hope in people on earth. Always place your main hope in me. Follow my will as best as you can and when your earthly family and friends fail you, do not despair, I am always near you and will never fail you. Stand by me and stand on my word as your only hope of glory and I will help you reach the all-satisfying success and shores of Heaven. Never lose sight of this—your main hope should always be in me. Nothing will happen in your life today that I can't handle.

The Response:

My Lord and my hope, I praise you and I give thanks to you for sending angels to watch over me during the night and for waking me this morning to see another day. As I live out this day no matter what comes my way, all of my hope will be in you. I ask that you would help me to prove this hope by my commitment to follow your will in all that happens to me today. I will deal with each and every event today as you desire and dictate. Today, I pledge to place all of my hope in you. Do with me as you see fit. You are the only one who knows and seeks my divine welfare. My hope is built on nothing less but Jesus' blood and righteousness. On Christ the solid rock I shall forever stand. Amen.

Day 133

The Reading:

Proverbs 16:17-20, "The path of the upright leads away from evil; whoever follows that path is safe. Pride goes before destruction, and haughtiness before a fall. It is better to live humbly with the poor than to share plunder with the proud. Those who listen to instruction will prosper; those who trust the Lord will be happy."

The Revelation:

Good morning my child and welcome to another day under the Heavens. I pray you will receive this day and enjoy it as a divine gift. It is very important that you keep your confidence tempered with a healthy fear of my justice. Don't be like the people in the world whose confidence comes from their pride. Such people only deceive themselves. If they only knew the horrible and terrible risk they were taking, they would be terrified. Unlike the people of the world, I want you to have a healthy self-confidence and make sure your confidence is rooted and grounded only in the facts. One fact to remember is without me you can do nothing. Your self-reliance will be only as good as it comes from a strong confidence and faith in me. There is a mistaken idea with the people in the world; they believe their greatness come from their own ability. Then there are those who believe they are strong enough to face any situation of sin. At times, those who were most respected and admired by the world were in great danger because they forgot their human weaknesses. Remember, temptations are not sin. In fact, they are blessings in disguise because they will help you realize how weak you are. On the other hand, never place yourself in the pathway of any temptation. If you love danger, you will have only yourself to blame if you get caught and perish in it. Never trust yourself too far or you will be flirting with temptation. Please be forewarned that over-confidence is dangerous. God will not bless foolishness and pride is foolishness. Always trust and depend on me and I will give you the wisdom to avoid sin. Nothing will happen in your life today that I can't handle.

The Response:

O Lord, my God and my deliverer, I greet you with words of joy and thanksgiving for blessing me to see this, another day. I ask you to lead and guide me throughout this day. As I also engage this day and its challenges, teach me how to acknowledge and avoid sin. Help me to realize that when I take risks with temptation, I am only being presumptuous. I seek to do and follow your will today and not my own. I want to avoid any and every thing that will draw me closer to sin. I pray that I will not offend you with pride of my own ability but please you by trusting in your daily guidance. Amen.

The Reflection: [What I heard the Holy Spirit speaking into my spirit during the past seven days and how it changed me or challenged me].

Day 134

The Reading;
Jeremiah 29:11-13, "For I know the plans I have for you," says the Lord. "They are plans for good and not for disaster, to give you a future and a hope. In those days when you pray, I will listen. If you look for me in earnest, you will find me when you seek me."

The Revelation:

Good morning my child and I pray all the graces of Heaven be yours for the asking today. Your spiritual growth and progress do not come from having a lot of joy and consolation. Your spiritual growth and progress come from being patient and humble and free from self-pity when things are going wrong. I want you to keep moving in your daily duties and never become careless when you no longer experience gratification in them. I want you to keep giving it your best in spite of any disinterest, disquietness or disgust in your spirit. Some people grow impatient and careless in serving me when things don't go as they wish. It is not always in your power to choose what you want during your earthly life. In spite of all of your plans, you will never be able to avoid all of the disappointments and setbacks that will come. Even the mistakes and sins of others, which give you a hard time are permitted by me for a good reason and purpose in your life. My child, I have a providential plan for you by which you will become great. I will only send what is best for you and the perfecting of your soul. If you will submit to and follow my will, you will gain the peace and joy that come from Heaven. If you rebel and resist, you will hurt and hinder only yourself. Heaven owes you nothing but you owe Heaven everything. You will always be in debt to me. Keep pressing on even when you don't feel like it. You will be proving your best love for me when you least feel like pleasing me. As long as you are following my holy will for your life, you are following my plan for your salvation. Always remember, I have a perfect plan for your life. Nothing will happen in your life today that I can't handle.

The Response:

My dearest Lord and Savior, thank you for guarding my life through the night. Thank you for waking me up this morning and starting me on my way today. I am blessed. I ask that you would make me the kind of servant and follower you would have me to be. I do not wish for my feelings or my moods to dictate or determine how I will or will not serve you today. No matter how I may feel or how much I may suffer, remind me that you are watching over me and that you have a plan for me. Help me to understand that even the evil that may come my way will have a purpose. I pray that my eyes will stay fixed on you and that I may fulfill your plan for my life throughout this day. You are my perfect peace and joy and never fading crown. Amen.

Day 135

The Reading:

Psalms 37:5-7, "Commit everything you do to the Lord. Trust him, and he will help you. He will make your innocence as clear as the dawn, and the justice of your cause will shine like the noonday sun. Be still in the presence of the Lord, and wait patiently for him to act. Don't worry about evil people who prosper or fret about their wicked schemes."

The Revelation:

Good morning my child; may the peace and joy of Heaven over take you all during this day. It is my desire for you to always do your best in following my word in your daily life. Never depend on human sympathy or admiration for succeeding in this life. You know what is right and I want you to execute it regardless of the pleasure or pain, which you may receive from it. Let your faith and your love become the strength that empowers and encourages you. If I always grant you divine consolation for every thing you do good, your life would not be a good example of true greatness. If the most selfish person would be awed and attracted to you, I want you to remain a humble servant of truth and integrity. I expect you to example the life of someone who is noble and true at all times. Discern what I desire and deserve of your life and try your best to give it to me daily. Forget about yourself and commit to my will and a holy and good life will be yours. Keep this thought in mind; any body can be cheerful and dedicated to me when I grant them my heavenly consolation. But real devotion and holy virtue towards me are seen when you don't have any feelings and inspirations yet you continue to do good. Your true love for me is not a mere sentiment. No. It is a holy conviction that you owe me everything. It is a persistent persuasion that I deserve the very best of your service daily. True greatness and devotion means loving my will and me more than your own imperfect ways and desires. Remember, nothing will happen in your life today that I can't handle.

The Response:

Dear Lord, my God and my all and all. I celebrate your goodness and your mercy for allowing me to live another day. Truly this is the day that you have made and I will rejoice in it every minute of this day. I will also commit to you and offer you my best and deepest love. Without you, I am well aware that I would have nothing and would be nothing. You have proven over and over again that your grace and generosity toward me has no limits. I pray that I may never refuse to be generous and all-giving to you. I desire to embrace your will in all things regardless of my own selfish likes or dislikes. I want to forever please you and accomplish your will in my life. Amen.

Day 136

The Reading:

Psalms 15:1-3, "Who may worship in your sanctuary, Lord? Who may enter your presence on your holy hill? Those who lead blameless lives and do what is right, speaking the truth from sincere hearts. Those who refuse to slander others or harm their neighbors or speak evil of their friends."

The Revelation:

Good morning my child and may the graces of Heaven shower down upon your heart and head as you enjoy and engage this day. Listen very carefully; do not believe everything that you hear about other people. Most people are inclined to judge their neighbors with prejudices. Their ill judgments often come from their own tastes, moods and selfish-love. You will usually come out better if you refuse to judge or accept the judgment by someone else's criticisms that you may hear. Many a person is condemned when they are unable to be present to defend mis-spoken criticisms. It is very sad and demonic but a lot of people only feel superior when they are criticizing others. They are compelled to exaggerate the faults of others. When you show interest in their demonic dialogue and discourse you are encouraging them to continue in their sinful talking. I want you to always show disapproval and discontent for all backbiting and backstabbing, if in no other way by your silence. Try to change the subject if possible and if you can't just simply walk away. Yes, everyone makes mistakes. The critic may even know how to do something better than the one being criticize and condemned but the motive or the intention of the one being criticize may not be known. No one has a right to reveal or ridicule another's hidden faults or shortcomings. The only time this is permissible is when you are defending the innocent or helping the guilty person correct his/her mistakes. Also, keep in mind that you may one day be the subject of the critic's criticism when you are not around. Speak up now for the one being criticized and talked about as you would want others to speak up for you. It is a divine virtue and duty. Nothing will happen in your life today that I can't handle.

The Response:

O Lord, my God and my King, I greet you with overflowing thanksgiving in my heart for granting me another day in this life. When my eyes greeted the dawning of this new day, I knew I had been blessed again. As I live out this day, grant me some of your grace that I may think well and speak well of my neighbors. Teach me to mind my own business. Remind me throughout this day of your mercy towards me that I may extend that same mercy to others. As I am forgiven so do I desire to forgive. Amen.

Day 137

The Reading:

1 Peter 5:8-9, "Be careful! Watch out for attacks from the Devil, your great enemy. He prowls around like a roaring lion, looking for some victim to devour. Take a firm stand against him, and be strong in your faith. Remember that your Christian brothers and sisters all over the world are going through the same kind of suffering you are."

The Revelation:

Good morning my child! This is another glorious day presented to you from Heaven. Please rejoice in it and accept it as a special gift. Hear me well today my child, always face the truth and never turn away from the facts. As long as you are in the world, you will never be free from trouble and temptation. The Bible emphasizes this fact over and over again: life on earth in a continuous trial. Therefore, you should never take temptation too lightly. You should always be on alert and on guard by engaging in on-going prayer and self-denial. When you do this the Devil will never be able to take you by surprise. The Devil never sleeps and he is always on the prowl; he is always roaming the earth; he is always searching for someone he can deceive and ultimately devour. Keep yourself girded up at all times and avoid those areas of life that I have warned you of and that are marked "danger." If you stay close to me in your daily walk, the Devil will think twice before he attempts to tempt you. When you get out of my will you become easy prey. The Devil uses all kinds of tricks and bait to seduce you and to lure you with temptation. Do not fall for them but remain strong and steadfast in the faith and I will deliver you in due time. The Devil is not your friend and nothing he suggests to you will benefit you. His objective is to destroy you. Only I desire to give you life and holy happiness. Be strong and keep watching. Nothing will happen in your life today that I can't handle.

The Response:

My Lord and my God; my very present help in the time of trouble and temptation. Thank you for guarding my life as I slept through the night. Thank you for waking me up this morning to see and live another day. As

I begin my daily journey, I pray that you will defend me against the Devil and his evil desires. Help me to be forever watchful and on guard against the Devil schemes that I may not yield to any of his temptations. Lead me today down paths of righteousness and holiness that I may not stray and become satanic prey. Protect me and preserve me for Heaven. Amen.

Day 138

The Reading;

Job 14:13-14, "I wish you would hide me with the dead and forget me there until your anger has passed. But mark your calendar to think of me again! If mortals die, can they live again? This thought would give me hope, and through my struggle I would eagerly wait for release."

The Revelation:

Good morning my child and may the many blessings of Heaven be yours today just for the asking. Whatever spiritual consolation comes your way today accept it gratefully. Remember, this is not something you earn; it is a free gift from God. I want you to dismiss any and all self-satisfaction from your heart. You should know with out any doubts that I am the only source of all that you enjoy. When you realize this eternal fact, you will gain a healthy humility whenever heavenly favors fall your way. Always beware of any vanity or pride. I desire that you abandon all foolish ideas of your own value and abilities. The hours of consolation will pass away and the time of trials and troubles will come again. Whenever consolation and comfort have vanished from you please do not become discouraged or disinterested in your divine duties. Keep up your prayers and good works. Humbly accept what is sent and be patient and diligent because the grace of comfort and consolation and enthusiasm will come again in due time. These periods of joy to sadness; happiness to heartaches are not unusual. Everyone who follows me must pass through them often in their lifetime. By your steadfastness and longsuffering, you will prove how much you love me. I want you to forever keep your eyes on me no matter what the situation or circumstance. Your season of suffering comes to give you a chance to improve your character and to introduce you to your faults and limitations. As you maintain your faithfulness and not submit to your impulses or emotions you will continue to move toward the home of peace and eternal happiness. Nothing will happen in your life today that I can't handle.

The Response:

O Lord, my Savior and my Healer, I greet you with gratitude this morning for sustaining my life to see another day. Whatever comes my way today, joy or sadness; success or failure, please remind me that they are all for a season.

Teach me how not to permit them to govern my actions in a sinful way. Let me not lose the fact that I am living for Heaven and all of my hardships and happiness are passing. As I pass through these seasons of suffering and setbacks, help me to remain focused and faithful. Grant me the favor of reaching Heaven someday no matter what my earthly experiences may be. Amen.

Day 139

The Reading:

Daniel 4:31-33, "While he was still speaking these words, a voice called down from heaven, `O King Nebuchadnezzar, this message is for you! You are no longer ruler of this kingdom. You will be driven from human society. You will live in the fields with the wild animals, and you will eat grass like a cow. Seven periods of time will pass while you live this way, until you learn that the Most High rules over the kingdoms of the world and gives them to anyone he chooses.' That very same hour the prophecy was fulfilled, and Nebuchadnezzar was driven from human society. He ate grass like a cow, and he was drenched with the dew of heaven. He lived this way until his hair was as long as eagles' feathers and his nails were like birds' claws."

The Revelation:

Greetings and the graces of Heaven are sent unto you this morning, my child. This is the sacred secret to all perfection—forget your self-interest and follow my will in all that you do. You desire what you think is good for you but you are often wrong in your desires. Only I want and know what is best for you and I am never wrong. If you want to be the kind of person that I want you to be, you must always submit and follow my will for your life. Study and learn my truths and leave the rest to me. You must learn that every human fault and frailty come from a mistaken self-love and pride. You will only overcome your shortcomings as far as you abandon your selfishness and pride and follow me. This you must do without any reservation or resistance. If you were to give all that you possess to the poor and yet have not given your heart to me, you have done nothing as far as eternity is concerned. Not even your greatest sacrifice will mean anything until you are determined to fight against your faults. There is no substitute for true virtue. This true virtue lies only in one thing and that is to accept and do my will in everything I desire. You are not as wise as you think you are. You do not know what is best for you. The truth is no one is richer and no one is happier than the one who does my will. You must empty yourself of pride and selfishness and place your daily life and desires in my hands. The key to obtaining heavenly peace is to surrender and submit your will to my will. Nothing will happen in your life today that I can't handle.

The Response:

Most gracious and ever loving Lord, I greet you with thanksgiving in my heart and on my lips for this gift of another day. Thank you for preserving my life. As I live out this day show me how to live a life of obedience and loyalty to your will. Teach me how to hate sin for what it is—self-deception and stupidity. I pray that I will forbid what is forbidden by you. It is my prayer to live my life today as a true follower of your will. You have proven your love for me and now I desire to prove my love for you by surrendering and submitting to your perfect will. Amen.

Day 140

The Reading:

Matthew 6:31-33, "So don't worry about having enough food or drink or clothing. Why be like the pagans who are so deeply concerned about these things? Your heavenly Father already knows all your needs, and he will give you all you need from day to day if you live for him and make the Kingdom of God your primary concern."

The Revelation:

Good morning my child and may the peace of Heaven be your constant companion all throughout this day. As you meditate during this day keep in mind that it is only in me that you will find what is best for you. There is nothing, absolutely nothing on planet earth far greater than what our heavenly Father has to offer you through me. It is only through me that you will ever obtain this perfect satisfaction and love. Plead and pray often to me for the grace you need to have that joy and holy happiness that you desperately desire. What I have to offer you is more than good health and beauty; is more than earthly glory and honor; is more than power and dignity; is more than human praise and admiration; is more than wealth and material possessions; is more than human consolation and appreciation; is more than whatever you dream of or think of. Don't you realize, that whatever you desire that is not of God is too little and too insufficient for you? I made you for myself and you will never find rest until you rest in me. My child, no matter what you like or love, unless it is our Heavenly Father, himself; it will never produce heavenly happiness in your soul. If you really want true rest and happiness seek me first and foremost and I will bless you with the joy beyond measure. Nothing will happen in your life today that I can't handle.

The Response:

Dear Lord, my God of grace and joy, I graciously greet you this morning with gratitude and thanksgiving for another anointed day on this earth. I submit to you that I cannot live for just a joy that is fastly fading away. Yes, I desire to experience a reasonable degree of earthly joy but I will never seek it through sin nor at the expense of forfeiting Heaven. The joy I do experience is a reflection of your joy in Heaven. It is my determined desire to seek the true joy that can only come from Heaven. As I live out this day, if any earthly attractions avail themselves to tempt me to sin, I pray that you will prompt me to remember your grace and the joy I have waiting on me in Heaven. Nothing on earth can ever be greater than that. Amen.

The Reflection: [What I heard the Holy Spirit speaking into my spirit during the past seven days and how it changed me or challenged me].